Dietrich

Dietrich

Malene Sheppard Skærved

HAUS PUBLISHING · LONDON

First published in Great Britain in 2003 by
Haus Publishing Limited
32 Store Street
London WC1E 7BS

Copyright © Malene Sheppard Skærved, 2003

The moral right of the authors has been asserted

'Academy Award' and 'Oscar' are Registered Trade Marks of
the Academy of Motion Picture Arts and Sciences

A CIP catalogue record for this book
is available from the British Library

ISBN 1-904341-13-6 (paperback)
ISBN 1-904341-12-8 (hardback)

Designed and typeset in Albertina at Libanus Press, Marlborough

Printed and bound by Graphicom in Vicenza, Italy

Front cover: photograph of Marlene Dietrich in *Blonde Venus*,
courtesy of the Marlene Dietrich Collection, Berlin
Back cover: illustration of Marlene Dietrich in *The Blue Angel*
courtesy of the Marlene Dietrich Collection, Berlin

Contents

Grief is a Private Affair[1]

Youth

THE DIETRICHS 1901–1910

In Schöneberg, a little outside Berlin, on Friday 27 December 1901, at a quarter past nine in the evening, Marlene Dietrich was born to Wilhelmina Elisabeth Josefine (1876–1945, *née* Felsing, known as Josefine) and Louis Erich Otto Dietrich (1868–1909). On the first workday after the Christmas holidays, her father registered her with the local authorities at the Schöneberg City Hall as Marie Magdalene Dietrich. She was nicknamed Leni.[2]

She was a very beautiful child, with reddish blonde hair, dimples and brilliant, deep-set pale blue eyes, resembling her father. Leni was second to an elder sister, Ottilie Josefine Elisabeth (called Liesel), born almost two years earlier in February 1900. From the earliest photographs, Leni's face leaps from the picture, even at this age, making her sister suffer by com-

Everyone knows how difficult it is to recall the early years of your life. We all have impressions, memories that do not always match reality, or that have blurred with time.[3]

parison. Everyone loved the adorable Leni, and Liesel knew it. Even then, she later remembered, men were crazy about Leni – they nicknamed her *Goldchen* (the little golden one).[4]

Immediately after their marriage in December 1898, the Dietrichs had moved into a modest flat at Sedanstrasse 53 (today, Leberstrasse 65) in Schöneberg. They may not have been affluent, but they were certainly comfortable, with a couple of servants and a telephone. After the five years of compulsory military duty (with no significant recorded distinctions and a pair of second-class medals), Louis was assigned a post as imperial police officer to Precinct 4. This was a reputable job, giving him and his family respectability

Left: At their wedding 1898; Louis Otto Dietrich, imperial police officer and Wilhelmina Elisabeth Josefine Felsing, daughter of a Berlin clockmaker

Right: The *Goldchen* Leni. Marlene Dietrich around age 5. With her blue eyes, her fair reddish hair and her engaging personality, she was adorable and adored

within the community, to be expected from families with their backgrounds.

Louis Dietrich's ancestors were French Huguenots who had settled in Brandenburg in the early 1800s. His father, Christian Dietrich (or Diedrich) (1820–98), had not lived to see his wedding. He too had a military background, and may even have worked as a policeman. Christian Dietrich trained as an upholsterer whilst in the military, and had worked as such in Schmargendorf. Later, he became an innkeeper in Angermünde, until he and his wife Ottilie Auguste Wilhelmine (1829–1918) retired to Eberswalde. She continued to live there until her death at the end of the First World War. Louis was one of eight surviving children; three more had not reached adulthood. One of his sisters stayed in Eberswalde taking care of their mother, whilst the others married. His brothers all found their way into good professions.

Josefine's family, the Felsings, had been prosperous clockmakers in Berlin since 1820. Their shop was named after the founder 'Conrad Felsing: Uhren-, Luxus- und Musik-Bazar' and was located at Unter den Linden 20, – the fashionable avenue in Berlin. In 1901 Josefine's father had just died. Josefine's younger (and only) brother, Willibald Albert Conrad (called Uncle Willi within the family) had taken over the family business. Aside from being a good crafts- and businessman, Uncle Willi had connections in the theatre and film world, which proved useful for his niece later on. In those days, he was renting out part of his shop to an optical instrument maker, Oskar Messter. There, in Willi's loft, Messter created Berlin's first working film studio, equipping the room with window-glass to allow in only the necessary light.

Everything augured well for the Dietrich family. There were good possibilities of a career in this pleasant town. Schöneberg was still separate from Berlin, and it was growing. In 1901, it had 90,000 inhabitants; over the next ten years, this grew to 170,000. In 1920, it was declared an official suburb of Berlin, along with several other districts. But in 1901, it was still a quiet and idyllic town with allotments, guesthouses, a chemical plant and others producing railway parts, cigars, soap, and paper. The town housed the headquarters of the Imperial Railway Company, located in Kolonnenstrasse, and a training ground for the military, an open green space conveniently close to the Dietrich family home.

When Thomas Eakins created a motion camera, George Eastman produced a roll of film and Louis Augustin Le Prince patented a machine to film and projected a sequence of images, motion pictures became a reality. The first commercial cinema opened in Pittsburg, USA, in 1905 and by 1906 film reels had reached 850 feet, running for 14 minutes. Short films, narratives and simple documentaries, were being shot across the world. Jesse Laskyin set up the first feature film company in Hollywood in 1913.

Between 1919 and 1933, the Weimar years, the German film industry arguably produced its most impressive collection of films to date, including: Robert Wiene's *The Cabinet of Dr Cagliari* (1919); Paul Wegener's *The Golem* (1920); Fritz Lang's *Destiny* (1921) and *Metropolis* (1925); F W Murnau's *Nosferatu* (1921) and *The Last Laugh* (1924); and G W Pabst's *Pandora's Box* (1928).

On the surface there were no reasons for the new family to be unhappy, but it soon became apparent that Louis was unsuited to marriage. Perhaps the Felsings had been right to be apprehensive about him. With her substantial dowry, Josefine had been a good match for Louis, but as time went by, she became disillusioned with her new husband. The young couple might have been in love at first, Josefine certainly was. But, after the birth of his two daughters, Louis's attention began to wander and he lost all interest, leaving Josefine and the girls alone for much of the time.

Louis was a handsome man; he had had many love affairs before he married, and was soon back to his old ways. His parents had encouraged him to marry, vainly hoping that a loving and devoted wife and children would settle him down and put an end to his philandering. They were disappointed. Josefine, however, never stopped loving him.

Infidelity was one thing, but Louis was also idling professionally. At each departmental exam he was demoted a rank at the police precinct. Eventually, he was at the foot of a list of twelve men with a mark of merely *Ausreichend* (sufficient).[5] The Dietrich family had often moved to accommodate the subsequent reduction in his income. By the time their daughters, Leni and Liesel were six and eight years-old respectively, the Dietrichs were in their fourth home. For the first years of marriage, the family moved together. But by 1906, Louis and Josefine were listed at separate addresses. The marriage may well have ended with separation, had Louis not fallen ill with a mysterious disease. It was never spoken of, and his young daughters were kept ignorant of his condition. Confronting her own death years later, Dietrich remembered being paraded in front of the hospital windows. *I always thought [my father] had syphilis and it went to his head,*[6] she told her daughter, but was reluctant to elaborate or explain further.

In 1907, Louis was undergoing frequent treatments for syphilis in a sanatorium. That year, he moved with Josefine and the girls into a house at Akasienalle 48. This must have been an unusual, perhaps even pleasant time for the girls. Their new house had a garden with a swing, and their father (before being permanently confined to hospital) was at home, albeit ill and in considerable pain. The cure for syphilis was still in its primitive stages; Louis was taken ill shortly before an effective treatment was available. He died on 5 August 1908, in a sanatorium for the mentally disturbed at Nussbaumallee 38. The story told to the Dietrich daughters was that their father had died from a heart attack, after falling off a horse. (Dietrich's later neurotic cleaning and sterilizing, particularly of toilets, seems to have stemmed from a fear of her father's illness.)

In 1909, at the age of 33, Josefine was a widow. She stayed in Schöneberg, moving to a new address, Tauentzienstrasse 13, with her daughters. With her widow's pension, and occasional help from her mother Elisabeth and brother Willi, Josefine raised her daughters, determined to live according to her own high Prussian standards, however difficult this might prove.

Liesel and Leni had both been enrolled at the Augusta Victoria School for Girls a couple of years before the death of their father. Prior to them starting school, at the relatively early age of five, their mother had already taught them to read and write German, some elementary French and English, along with sewing and other domestic skills.

Josefine was bringing up her daughters in accordance with the exacting standards and expectations of the time; preparing them for marriage. The Prussian ideal of womanhood, of *Kinder, Küche und Kirche* (children, cooking, and the Church) was unquestioned. When Dietrich looked back at her childhood, she remembered the strict discipline of her Prussian mother, and a world filled with learning and culture.

The girls continued to be taught at home, by private tutors. In addition to their school classes, they studied literature, languages, music and housekeeping. Josefine kept them occupied at all times. They went to school from 8am to 1pm, then ate lunch for half an hour before an hour's homework. After that there were two hours of private tuition, followed by two more hours of homework. They ate dinner at 7.30pm and were in bed about 8 o'clock. The girls also had a weekly gym class and French and English lessons. Leni, who displayed an aptitude for music, took extra classes. She studied the piano and violin, and would later add the lute.

Liesel was a bookish child and enjoyed school. Leni, though younger than most of the girls in her class, was ahead academically. In spite of this natural ability, she found school boring and had a difficult time making friends. She remembered her first couple of years at school as a lonely time. Long afterwards, a fellow student recalled Dietrich as 'the shyest girl in our school. She was diffident and nervous, and did not enjoy anything very much. I do not think in any way she was an outstanding pupil. She always seemed to find a place in a corner, like a little grey mouse. Nobody had the slightest idea she would amount to anything.'[8]

Leni regretted her physical similarity to her dissolute father and wanted to be more like her mother. She sensed the pain Louis had brought to her mother and did not want to be the one reminding Josefine of her late husband. To Josefine's credit, she never denigrated the memory of Louis in front of his children. A child who looks like her father, she reassured Leni, is a lucky child. But Leni had inherited more than her father's looks; aspects of his character began to show themselves in her behaviour. This could hardly have been what Josefine was hoping to see in a daughter. As opposed to the shy, well-mannered, and obedient Liesel, Leni was wild and flirtatious, the 'boy' of the family. Josefine suspected that her youngest daughter was compensating for her absent father. She called herself 'Paul' (with the

French pronunciation), taking on the role of the male head of the household. Josefine played along.

Although Josefine was imperturbable and always behaved appropriately, she found it more difficult to keep a sense of perspective when it came to her daughters. They feared and needed her in equal measure. It was a feeling that was to last them both for the rest of their lives. Dietrich later described her mother as *'not kind, not compassionate, [but] unforgiving and inexorable . . . The rules were . . . ironclad, immovable, unalterable.'*[10] Almost as if to please her absent husband, Josefine raised her girls within quasi-military rules of logic and duty. She was an officer's wife, and any soldier would have been impressed by the way in which she managed her daughters.

EDUARD VON LOSCH 1910–1916

Louis died when Leni was only seven years old. Although she remembers a secure childhood, she is unlikely to have been aware of the family's economic circumstances as Louis's career declined or in the aftermath of his death. Josefine's financial position, even with the help from her family, was increasingly desperate. She needed money if she was going to keep up the appearance of middle-class wealth and leisure and so took a job in a glove factory. Then she met Lieutenant Eduard von Losch (1875–1916). A classmate of Dietrich recalled that at first Josefine became a 'glorified housekeeper'. Later she married him.[11]

Eduard von Losch was born in Dessau into an ennobled Brandenburg family. He was a year younger than Josefine and a first lieutenant in the Grenadier Guards. In 1913 he was promoted to Captain. He had studied law for a few terms

Eduard von Losch with two of his three sisters, (*left*) Alwine and (*right*) Valeska (Tante Valli), 1907 in Munich before abandoning his studies and joining the military. His father, Ferdinand von Losch (1843–1912) had been a Royal Colonel in the Prussian Army and his mother Agnes von Losch (*née* Trotha) (1850–1941) came from a well-connected family. He often entertained the Dietrich girls with stories of his time spent fighting in China during the Boxer Rebellion. He had filled his house with a fine collection of Chinese furniture and artefacts and continued to pursue his interest in the Orient. Upon his return to Germany, he studied Chinese at Berlin University. Two of his three sisters had married extremely well and it was expected that he would do the same. As Eduard spent so much time away on military manoeuvres, it is likely he would have needed a housekeeper. Josefine Dietrich was a friend, someone he could trust, and perhaps he felt some responsibility for Josefine and her daughters.

The circumstances of Josefine Dietrich's first meeting with Eduard von Losch are unclear. It is most likely that Louis Dietrich had introduced his wife to Eduard when they were in the army. A family rumour – started by Dietrich's cousin Hasso Conrad Felsing, – suggested that Eduard and Josefine had met through Josefine's work for the Red Cross. However, they both had many military connections that could have performed the introduction. It was even implied that their relationship was a 'white marriage' – an arrangement not unusual at the time – and that the couple were never shared anything beyond a surname. The least likely scenario is that they started a love affair whilst Josefine was still married to Louis, as this would have contradicted everything she stood for.

Dietrich always described her mother as extraordinarily beautiful, and her grandmother as even more so. Although Louis was supposedly the philanderer, Dietrich could have inherited some of her allure and romantic nature from her mother as well. Josefine was, after all, the only parent around to influence her children. There can be no doubt that this single mother of two daughters, with her formidable and stern personality, was also very intelligent, resourceful, and really quite remarkable. *She possessed a kind of natural nobility,* Dietrich later explained. *Her behaviour, her authority, her intellectual attitude were those of an aristocrat. Just looking at her made it easy to respect her.* [12] Eduard could not help but fall in love with this exceptional woman, despite family resistance.

Josefine had moved herself and the two girls into Eduard's house at Kaiserallee 219/220 before she married him. The couple might have presented themselves as husband and wife for the sake of propriety, Josefine's honour, his career, or just to frustrate the gossips. The outbreak of war in Europe changed everyone's attitude to marriage as thousands of young couple hurriedly exchanged vows. There was much as stake as pensions had to be secured for those who may be widowed. Eduard and Josefine would have felt these pressures all the more with two children to support.

According to a diary kept by a family member, the couple married in private in August 1914, just as war was declared. Eduard's mother Agnes von Losch witheld her blessing, but Josefine's daughters were happy to have a new father. By the time von Losch left for war, Leni was mostly calling him *Vatel* (Dad), and only occasionally noted him as 'Losch' in her journals, indicating that Eduard had accepted parental responsibility for Liesel and Leni. The girls would spend the school holidays with Uncle Willi and his family in Wandlitz or with Eduard in Dessau. [13]

Through Eduard, Josefine was introduced to a more refined society. Although his relatives may initially have been apprehensive about the marriage, Eduard's sisters soon grew to like Josefine and her daughters and regarded them as family. His sister, Valeska (called Tante Valli), who was married to Otto Varnhagen, and therefore one of the wealthiest members of the family was a particular favourite of Leni's. One Easter she presented Leni was with a diary and encouraged her to use it as a secret friend to whom she could confide her innermost feelings. Dietrich did as she was told, establishing a lifelong habit, of consigning her secrets to the pages of her diaries. Events or daily drudgeries that were too dull to excite her imagination were excluded. As any girl at the age of eleven who has been told to record her feelings would, Leni filled the pages of her diaries with gossip, youthful imaginings of love and melancholy yearnings. Domestic life, and ominous world events had yet to take on the significance they would hold for her in years to come – they rarely made it onto the pages. Leni's diaries became her consoling refuge and a repository of her dreams. From the opening pages,

Facts are unimportant. I never kept a diary. I was always indifferent to the glitter of fame. I found it troublesome, crippling and dangerous. Unlike most actors and actresses, I hate to behave like a star . . . That is how I am, and I can't be otherwise.[15]

they reveal a natural curiosity for who she was and, more importantly, a desire to explore her future potential. Her craving to love and be loved developed into the ambition which would drive her onwards. She began to create the passionate and romantic 'Marlene Dietrich' of future years.

Now that Leni was almost a teenager and growing up fast, she needed another name – Leni was the name of a little girl. Her full name, 'Mary Magdalene' (named after the prostitute who anointed Jesus's feet with oil), was hardly appropriate for a blossoming young beauty – however pertinent it would have been for so many of her future film roles. She wanted a name which would both reflect and define her, her unique creation. On the cover of a school notebook, Dietrich combined the first three letters of Marie with the last four of Magdalene and created the name *Marlene Dietrich*. She began using it exclusively from then on, and as most people never knew her by any other, she would eventually claim that it was her real name.[15]

However Josefine might try to ignore the fact, her daughter displayed a rare precocity. She spent most of her time flirting and falling in love. From her teenage years, her emotional life was turbulent. She worshipped women obsessively, and loved men in a passionate and self-subordinating manner. The impending war only served to reaffirm this pattern. Men were absent, aside from brief passionate visits home. Women were around to share each other's grief and support one another.

In August 1914, Germany went to war. Hundreds of thousands of men enlisted, but as the war dragged on, their early eagerness dimmed. The cosmopolitan world, in which Marlene had grown up, faded away. She regretted the loss of the international culture which had surrounded her before the war. Suddenly, the English, French, and Russians were enemies of Germany. Most memorably her French teacher, Madame Breguard had been obliged to leave, and there were no more English girls in the school. Like every woman, Marlene contributed in her way to the war effort, supporting the troops by knitting and sewing, playing her violin 'for Germany' and singing patriotic songs.

WORLD WAR I

1914
28 June, Archduke Franz Ferdinand of Austria-Hungary is assassinated in Sarajevo.
28 July, Austria-Hungary declares war on Serbia.
1 August, Germany (allied with Austria-Hungary) declares war on Russia (Serbia's ally).
3 August, Germany declares war on France and invades Belgium.
4 August, Britain delivers ultimatum to Germany, demanding respect for Belgian neutrality. German troops continue to advance through Belgium towards Paris. Britain declares war on Germany (and consequently on Germany's allies).
6–9 September, German advance is stopped in the Battle of the Marne. Trench warfare ensues.

1915
April/May, heavy fighting near Ypres, with little movement of the front despite huge losses on both sides.

1916
21 February–21 July, 'Hell of Verdun': after initial success heavy losses force the Germans to stop fighting.
24 June–26 November, Battle of the Somme: Anglo-French attempts to break through German lines fail.
24 October–16 December, French retake the Fortress of Verdun.

1917
February/March, German retreat.
6 April, USA declares war on Germany.

1918
March–July, German Spring attack leads to minor territorial gains.
8 August, first tank attack at Amiens. German army retreats to its 'Siegfried Line'.
11 November, armistice.

1919
18 January, start of negotiations leading to the signing of the Peace Treaty of Versailles, 28 June.

On 6 August 1914, Eduard was sent to the Western Front. In September, he sustained a wound to his right arm and was sent to recover in a hospital in Braunschweig. Josefine and the girls spent three weeks in a nearby guesthouse to be close to him. After Eduard's recovery he returned to the front. Soon, every able-bodied man had been conscripted, including most of the Dietrich and the von Losch families. Uncle George, Uncle Willi and Tante Valli's husband, Uncle Otto, were all awarded the Iron Cross for bravery.

Eduard insisted that for safety's sake Josefine take the girls out of Berlin and to his family in Dessau. There, they could help his mother. The war was beginning to drain the country's resources; food was increasingly scarce in the cities, there was little milk, meat, or vegetables to be had. The food most commonly available was turnips, which slowly turned everyone's skin a sickly yellow. (According to Dietrich, she was the only one who did not to lose her lovely, clear skin.)

It was at this time that Liesel and Marlene began using the name 'von Losch'. Although Josefine and Eduard were married, he never legally adopted the girls. Nevertheless his role as parent was officially recognized. According to the school protocol for 1916–17, Marlene registered at the Antoneten Lyzeum, Dessau as 'Magdalena von Losch'.[16] For Marlene, life continued in Dessau more or less as it had in Berlin; school, homework, and violin lessons. But her need for independence increased. Soon, Josefine was worrying about her daughter's flirtatiousness and appetite for boys. The war had not taken away all the boys of Marlene's age. In the evenings after homework, Marlene would *bummel* (Berliner slang for strolling) the streets with her friends on 'boy-hunts'.[17] She fell in and out of love carelessly and would often end up kissing boys in dark alleyways. Josefine had good reason to be concerned, and intended to put a stop to this immoral conduct, but tragically, other matters would distract her from Marlene's adolescent rebellion.

In 1916, Eduard was sent to the Eastern Front. Josefine tried to meet him *en route* but failed. On 20 June, he was shot in the arm whilst serving on the Lithuanian front. This time the injury was so serious that an amputation became unavoidable. Josefine used every connection she had to gain a special permit to travel to his hospital in Mirosławiec. Unfortunately, during the operation he contracted blood poisoning; he died in his wife's arms on 16 July.

Marlene had lost another father figure, though like Louis, Eduard had been noticeable more for his absence than for his presence. The loss of both these men created in Marlene an idealized memory of a father – a tall man dressed in uniform with boots, and smelling of leather and horses.

To her mind, everything – her behaviour, her education, even the rituals of daily life within the home – was dominated by the needs of men. In reality, Dietrich had lived most of her young life with only a sense of men, rather than with their actuality. Men as fathers, husbands and protectors were of so little consequence to her that when Uncle Otto was killed

Most of my schoolmates didn't have fathers. We didn't miss them: we hardly knew they were gone. We lived in a women's world: the few men with whom we came into contact were old or ill, not real men. The genuine men were at the front; they were fighting until they fell. After the war, many years went by before men existed again. Our life among women had become such a pleasant habit that the prospect that the men might return at times disturbed us – men who would again take the sceptre in their hands and again become lords in their households. [18]

in 1915, the 13-year-old Marlene barely registered the tragedy in her journal. Instead she noticed how beautiful Tante Valli looked in her black widow's dress with its white collar. Now, with Eduard gone, and her Uncle Max's zeppelin shot down over England, the list of fallen soldiers lengthened by the day, Marlene could no longer avoid the reality of the war. The men were not returning and Josefine had had little time to show Eduard how much she loved him.

Eduard's sisters, particularly Tante Valli, remained kind to Josefine and her daughters, but his mother never accepted her as part of the family. After only 18 months in Dessau, Josefine moved her daughters back to Kaiseralle in Berlin, where the girls started at the Viktoria-Luisen-Schule (today the Goethe Gymnasium) in the autumn of 1917. There they studied German, French, English, history, geology, religion, maths, physics, chemistry, music, gymnastics, and needlework. Two years later Marlene earned her *Abschlußzugnis* (the certificate of completion given at the end of secondary school). Liesel stayed on; she would need her *Abitur*, the higher degree, to be able to go to university.[19]

It's so much nicer if one has someone – it makes you feel so pretty … I wear my hair up, and when something special is happening I let a curl fall MARLENE DIETRICH, Berlin, 18 June 1917[20]

Josefine was a widow again, but this time financially secure with two pensions, a noble name, and a foothold in society. In 1917, fulfilling a wish of her late husband and to pacify the von Losch family, Josefine bought Marlene her first good violin. It cost 2,000 marks and was sold to her by one of her violin professors. Marlene's training as a professional violinist was now in earnest. Liesel was meant for books, Marlene for music.

Back in Berlin and living again in Eduard's large house, Marlene now had a room of her own, a small attic above the bathroom, cosily decorated with 'a big rug, pink curtains and electric light'.[21] She practised the violin for six hours a day and played first violin

As a violinist in a school production in her black sports trousers, her mother's riding coat and lace shirt, October 1917

in the school orchestra. In 1917, she played the violin in the school play in male attire. As it was the anniversary of the execution of the Hapsburg Emperor Maximilian of Mexico, the play carried a Mexican theme. In several of the pictures, she is clearly showing off by posing playing high on the G-string – a particularly difficult position. Marlene was obviously eager for everyone to see how fine a virtuoso she was.

Although she was still getting good marks in school, academia could not fulfil her. The women around her were all in mourning for their men and affection was a thing of the past. Marlene became dissatisfied. There had to be more to life than the studious and quiet world of a widow's daughter; she longed for love, romance and attention. At this time, her love for women seems to have been even more intense than her feelings for boys. In the summer of 1917, she had fallen for the beautiful, young and playful Countess Gersdorf. She wooed her desperately, but the Countess simply did not understand. On 14 August 1917, Marlene wrote: *How indulgent love is. Love suffers, tolerates, hopes. Her picture is in my locket. Sometimes my love is like a baby's, although it is serious, like a grown-up. It is the kind of love I could feel for a man. What a shame, really, that she doesn't understand me, she only thinks it's a simple crush. I call it a crush myself, but in reality it's not that easy. The whole situation! A crush one can forget easily, but one's love*

COUNTESS GERSDORF

not.[22] Real people, even women it turned out, were fickle; they too left you behind. But what Marlene could not get from her crushes, she found at the movies.

Most of the girls at Marlene's school would have adored Henny Porten, a German screen idol at the time. (Her house still stands in Berlin and is now a restaurant.) Naturally, Marlene also worshipped and loved Porten; she pursued this new-found passion aggressively. Her diary entries during 1917 and 1918 are filled with her obsessive longings and sexual fantasies for the actress. She sent off for signed photographs and waited outside Porten's Berlin apartment to give her flowers and cakes, to let the star know how much she was loved and adored. She even serenaded

Henny Porten (1890–1960) was a German actress. She began her career in 1906 with the film pioneer, Oskar Messer. She appeared in 150 silent and 17 sound films, most often portraying abandoned or seduced women suffering inconsolably.

her at her front door playing the violin, leaving Porten slightly bemused by all of the attention. On a school trip to Mittenwald, Marlene, discovering that Henny Porten was holidaying nearby with her psychiatrist husband, decided to make yet another appearance. Getting up early in the morning, she took the first train to the resort of Garmisch and made her way to the couple's balcony to serenade her idol for a second time. Flattered, but disturbed to see the same girl from Berlin yet again, Porten slammed her bedroom windows, shutting out the sight of her biggest fan. Marlene hardly minded, as she had made her admiration known. Her adoration was to last years.

Still searching for romance, and after much begging, Marlene was allowed to take up the lute. She was given another teacher. She adorned her lute with trailing ribbons and spent hours singing sentimental Bavarian and Austrian folksongs in the fashion of her idol Henny Porten. Later she would write: *I was head over heels in love with [my lute] and hugged it every night before going to bed. I felt a little guilty for not feeling the same tenderness for my violin. Maybe it touched me because it was smaller.*[23]

Years later, in an interview from 1931, called 'My First Love', Dietrich was finally able to publicly declare her love for Porten. In one of her films, Henny Porten used a Gobelin-embroidered pillow which Marlene herself had made and sent her. So the whole cinema could hear her, she exclaimed, *Mum, look, she fell on my cushion.*[24] The story perhaps shows more wishful thinking, testament to Dietrich's romantic nature and hope of Porten's acceptance of her affections, than actual fact. Dietrich

Dietrich in Bavarian Lederhosen, and her beloved lute with her mother and sister, Liesel, around 1918

was a master storyteller; if a 'white lie' served her purpose, she did not hesitate to use it.

With all the other anxieties of living through the summer of 1918, this pining for love depressed Marlene enough to make her ill. Her doctor informed her 'that the muscle of her heart [had] weakened' and she needed to rest and take special sulphur baths.[21] That gave her just what she craved, her mother's attention and a romantic 'cure'. Marlene was soon well again.

On 11 November 1918, Germany surrendered. Those men who were not dead were returning home, crippled mentally and physically. No one wanted to talk about the war, and the women did not know what to think or how to ask. All that Marlene could do was to reconcile herself to the nation's anger and to lament her own insignificant role within the disaster. *Why must I experience these terrible times? I did so want a golden youth and now it turned out like this! I am sorry about the Kaiser and all the others . . . What does the nation want? They have what they wanted, haven't they? Oh, if I were a little bit happy, things wouldn't be so difficult to bear. Maybe soon a time will come when I will be able to tell about happiness again – only happiness.*[26]

Josefine too wanted a 'golden childhood' for her daughters and even more, to try to preserve their innocence and sense of equilibrium for just a little longer. She rented a house in Springeberg to get her family away from the post-war confusion and rioting in Berlin. She and the girls now had somewhere safe to go during holidays and weekends. They soon found that they were not the only ones going there. Marlene was ecstatic. She was surrounded by boys, fêted and pursued, just as she had always dreamed. Now Josefine really had reasons to worry, if she was hoping to keep her daughter pure and innocent. Her daughter's own words reveal just how far Marlene was prepared to go. She wrote in her journal: *For the moment, they are all crazy about me ... I can't decide between them ... Till now I have had the strength to say 'No' as it got to the very moment. But that is getting hopeless. They are all alike: he 'can't control himself anymore,' and, as my feelings arouse his, it is no longer a love of youth. It is too late for that.*[28] Josefine had to step in. She had often threatened to send Marlene off to boarding school if she did not end her 'boy crazy' behaviour. Now she acted on it. Grandmother Felsing had died recently and left Josefine her share of the shop's profits. As Germany's inflation began to race, the money provided by a business was always good news, while any savings and investments were wiped out. Marlene was finishing school and there were no plans for her to go to university. She needed a place to continue her music training. With Berlin in chaos, the provincial Saxonian town of Weimar seemed ideal. Josefine decided that a conservative girls' school would be able to discipline her daughter where she had failed.

In the 1960s Marlene Dietrich wrote: *Like other young girls at that time, I knew little about what was going on outside the narrow frame of my little world ... [We] had no interest whatsoever in politics or political events...[We] were affected only by the daily happenings in [our] immediate circle: the household, personal achievement, weddings and children. Even as we grew older and inflation hit the country, our attitude didn't change ... Our own problems seemed to be far more important, and we weren't in the least inclined to ask ourselves about the reasons for the insecurity that ripped Germany apart in the 1920s.*[27]

Kisses. Don't waste them. But don't count them.[24]

Weimar

1919—1921

Weimar shaped Dietrich for life, but not in the manner that Josefine had hoped; Marlene soon came to relish the independence her years in boarding school gave her. The world Josefine knew, for which she had prepared her daughters, had been destroyed by the war. Women, particularly the younger ones, now knew that it was possible to survive without men. Regardless of how much it appalled the older generation, youth was learning how to make new rules on its own.

At the beginning of her residence in Weimar, Marlene had trouble adjusting. This was her first time away from home, and she was lonely. She missed her sister, her mother and, of course, all the boys who had loved her. Marlene roomed with five other girls in Frau Alberti's boarding house. The landlady assumed responsibility over all the girls and reported back to Josefine. Marlene was finally studying music full-time at the *Musikhochschule* (music academy), as well as taking private violin lessons with the Swiss Hofkapell-meister (court music director), Dr Robert Reitz. Although he was married with children, he proved to be a bit of a rogue.

> *I am so unhappy because I don't have any-body who loves me. I am so used to being loved. Miss Arnoldi, the headmistress, wants to change me according to her standards and Mutti seems to agree with that and be happy about it. As everyone is working hard to change me, I hope something will come out of it that will please Mutti.*
>
> MARLENE DIETRICH Diary, Weimar, 10 October 1920 [30]

Marlene found her feet and made friends quickly enough. The city was considered the birthplace of German classical literature as Johann Wolfgang von Goethe and Friedrich Schiller had lived and worked there 100 years earlier. The romantic and cultural ambience appealed to Marlene. She went to concerts, plays and exhibitions with her friends. Soon she was mingling with a rapidly growing artistic set that gathered in Weimar in the beginning of the 1920s. Through friends at the boarding house, she even managed an introduction to the notorious beauty and composer Alma Mahler-Gropius, the wife of the Bauhaus founder, Walter Gropius. He had brought a group of avant-garde artists, architects, painters, and designers to Weimar, setting up what became the 'Staatliches Bauhaus Weimar' just around the time Marlene arrived. Its role, he declared, was to 'raze the arrogant wall between artist and artisan'.[31] Alma, the widow and muse of the composer Gustav Mahler, the one-time mistress of Gustav Klimt and Oskar Kokoschka, intrigued Marlene as much as she did everyone else. Not much came from their meeting, but Alma Mahler-Gropius whispered to her hostess, 'What eyes this one has.'[27] This was enough, however, to satisfy Marlene; someone worldly and important had noticed her.

Marlene finally managed to lose her virginity in Weimar. Flirting and music had always been linked for her and she shocked her classmates as she left for her lessons with Dr Reitz in outfits of

WEIMAR REPUBLIC

Founding years 1918–19

29 October, mutiny of German sailors is the start of a revolution. 9 November, Emperor Wilhelm II abdicates and goes into exile, a republic is declared and the leader of the Social Democratic party, Friedrich Ebert assumes governmental powers. 11 November, armistice ends World War I. In December the Berlin congress of councils of workers and soldiers decides to hold elections for a constitutional assembly, which convenes in Weimar in February 1919. Ebert is elected President by this National Assembly.

Crisis Years 1919–23

The nationalist bourgeoisie and the army are as much opposed to the republic as left-wing extremists. Strikes and communist unrest, political murders, and two putsch attempts threaten the young republic. A quick succession of governments is unable to rein back inflation and the economic situation is worsened by reparation payments forced on Germany by the Treaty of Versailles. French and Belgian troops occupy the Ruhr industrial valley and seize the mined coal 'in lieu' of unpaid reparations.

sheer chiffon. Dr Reitz did not send her home to dress appropriately, as Josefine would have hoped. Instead he eventually took her suggestive outfit as a hint and had sex with her on the sofa in his studio. *He groaned, heaved, panted. Didn't even take his trousers off. I just lay there on that old settee, the red plush scratching my behind, my skirts over my head. The whole thing, very uncomfortable,* Dietrich told her daughter many years later.[33] The event did not make it into her diary. Maybe it never happened or, more likely, the experience was simply too

Dietrich with an unknown admirer probably during her Weimar years

embarrassing and unpleasantly unromantic for Dietrich to want to record.

Her stories of her sexual exploits from her Weimar days later circled around Berlin. Her old friend from Vienna, Billy Wilder, used

Reaction Years 1924–30

Five elections never lead to clear majorities. In February 1925 Ebert dies and is succeeded by the World War I hero, Paul von Hindenburg, a monarchist. His election is a sign of the reactionary mood of the majority of the population. Successive governments become more and more dependent on emergency powers bestowed on them by the President. In the foreign policy sphere Gustav Stresemann achieves a rapprochement between France and Germany and her accession to the League of Nations.

Final Years 1930–33

In the general elections of September 1930, the extreme right and left parties score the biggest gains. The political spectrum is radicalized. President Hindenburg is re-elected in 1932, the same year that the Nazis become the strongest party in parliament. Adolf Hitler forms a coalition with the reactionary conservative parties and is sworn in as Reichskanzler (Chancellor) in January 1933. Using emergency powers, he is able to suspend the democratic rights of the individuals enshrined in the Weimar Constitution.

to entertain his dinner guests by having Dietrich chronicle her early love life. Recalling Marlene's conquests, he remembered the violin teacher, as well as another violinist and a piano player. When the gathered company seemed appropriately shocked, Dietrich would innocently say, *Oh, are we boring you?. . .* only to continue by adding, *And that was just the men . . .* 34

There is nothing unique about a woman sleeping her way up the rungs of the career ladder. What is unusual was Dietrich's control over these encounters; a control she appears to have exercised from very early on. She seems to have relished the attention and simply put up with the sex as an essential if undesirable part of assuring it. Later she would even allow old lovers back into her bed if they could serve some purpose. *[They] are so sweet when they ask, and then, they are so happy afterwards. So . . . you do it! . . . Don't you?* 35 She did not care much for the actual sex, only the wooing that preceded it and the devoted gratitude afterwards. The men (and later women) usually stimulated her in more ways than the merely sexual; often they were crucial to her artistic development. It is, however, difficult to believe that her sexual exploits did not occasionally hurt or belittle her. This, nonetheless, was a price she was prepared to pay.

THE ACTRESS 1921–1922

Marlene returned to Berlin in the autumn of 1921, to a city in turmoil. Inflation was affecting everything and everyone. As money devalued daily, Josefine had to accept that, as neither of her daughters would have a dowry to ensure a good marriage, they would have to work. When Liesel completed her studies, she accepted a job as a teacher, her financial independence allowing Marlene the luxury of continuing to study music. Although Marlene had not been accepted at the Berlin Hochschule für Musik (the Academy of Music), she was taking private classes with one of their most distinguished professors, Carl Flesch.

Regardless of her being a girl, Giuseppe Becce (Dean of Berlin's film orchestra and the composer of the silent score for F W Murnau's *Der Letzen Mann/The Last laugh*) hired Marlene as concert-mistress, and the only female member of the German Film Studio's Universum-Film-Aktiengesellschaft cinema orchestra. A silent movie could be accompanied by anything from an upright piano to an orchestra, small or big, depending on the size of the theatre. The orchestra was hired to travel with specific films as the musicians needed to know how to coordinate the score with the actions on the screen. The job required good timing combined with a well-developed sense of tempo, tone and control. Becce

Germany's industrial wealth was wiped out by World War I and the economy further crippled by reparation payments levied by the Treaty of Versailles. The republican government borrowed money, which led to hyper-inflation: in 1923, one US-dollar was worth 4.2 billion marks. People lived for the moment, and dances such as the Charleston flourished as Berlin established a reputation for decadence.

found Marlene 'highly gifted'.[34] but despite being completely satisfied with her work, he had to let her go. The men in the orchestra found her legs too distracting. More likely they were unable to accept being led by a woman. That seems to have finished Marlene's music career. Almost as if on cue (perhaps she needed a physical reason to stop), she got a tendon inflammation in her right hand. Flesch had had her practising unaccompanied Bach for eight hours a day and it had cramped up her hand. '[She] never liked Bach after that.'[37]

She was ordered by the doctor to rest her hand; even after months of not playing, she was allowed to work only on easy repertoire. Still, someone with Marlene's aptitude and stamina could have brought herself back to playing standard,

Had I begun the piano instead of the violin, I might have been a great concert pianist. Yet when I practised the violin, I became conscious of the difficulties and I entertained no illusions. Besides, the social prejudices of the day stood in the way of a career as a professional performer.[38]

had she wished it. Yet, there seemed to be little point if she was unable to play difficult music or indeed to perform in public. *I was the first to give up.* Dietrich explained later. *For my mother, it was one more broken*

dream. As for me, for the first time for a long while, I had nothing to do. [39]
With her new-found time and plenty of energy, Marlene devoured book after book, from Rilke to Goethe, everything she could get her hands on. And then, suddenly, she knew she would become an actress and combine the best of both worlds, performance with words. On stage as an actress, she could be everything at once – passionate, serious, sexy, sensual, intelligent, strong or submissive – there, perhaps, she would not be stopped by the constant restrictions she had encountered in the musical world. To her mother's horror, she decided to audition for the Max Reinhardt Drama School in Berlin. The only thing that appeased Josefine was that the good name of von Losch would not need to be sullied and Eduard's family could not be offended. Magdalene von Losch already had a legitimate stage name, Marlene Dietrich.

Maybe someone will have the kindness to marry me and then my career as an artist can end – but practise for years just to play at home? How could one have the strength to pursue such a thing.
Weimar, 21 October 1920 [40]

She had no acting training, no control of her voice or stage-craft, just a burning desire to succeed. She had chosen a passage from a Reinhardt-produced play, *Der Tor und der Tod (Death and the Fool)* for the initial audition. Perhaps it brought her luck. She was considered talented enough to make it to the second round. This time, she chose Margaret's prayer (in later versions, Gretchen) from Goethe's *Faust*. This sublime piece was certainly beyond her. She kept falling enthusiastically to her knees, until someone threw her a pillow. The provocative gesture confused her and she was unable to respond. As Dietrich told it later, the pillow had been thrown by Reinhardt himself, who, indifferent to her thespian efforts, called out for her to lift her skirt and show off her legs. In another version of the story, he told her that even had she shed real tears, she had not made him do so. These are all great tales. The fact is that Reinhardt was in Vienna at the time of the audition and that he never auditioned prospective students. By the time Max Reinhardt was in Hollywood (due to the war) and his fame considerably less than that of 'his most famous student', he had sense enough not to contradict her. Marlene Dietrich was never accepted as a student at the Max Reinhardt Drama School. [41]

The inconvenience of a mere refusal was not going to stop her; Marlene had been rejected before. She knew there were other and perhaps even better ways to study than as part of the establishment. Using her connections, she convinced a friend to arrange a backstage introduction to the notorious cabaret star, Rosa Valetti. Intrigued enough by Marlene's voice, despite finding her talent a little too 'natural', Valetti took pity on her and set up a meeting with Felix Holländer, a Reinhardt administrator. He passed her on to another one of the school's administrators, Dr Berthold Held. Along with a fellow hopeful, Grete Mosheim, Marlene started private lessons with him. (Mosheim later became an important actress in German theatre and film.) If the two girls had to hand out sexual favours to get this far, they accepted it as a necessary price. And they had each other with whom to giggle their way through.

In the autumn of 1921, Marlene moved out of the family home. She had met Gerda Huber – an aspiring journalist who offered her a place in her flat. Soon they were inseparable, though from all accounts, just as friends. 'Marlene preferred to spend long hours indoors,' Gerda Huber later said. '[She] cared little for dancing or amusement. She became the pet of the landlady, Trude, because she was always buzzing about in the kitchen helping to prepare the meat and puddings, and because she kept her room in perfect order.' [42]

All this soon changed: Grete Mosheim remembers Marlene in 'fine stockings and beautiful high-heeled shoes. She looked great at seven in the morning; who knows how she could afford it?' [43] The answer was: Tante Jolly. While Marlene was in Weimar, her Uncle Willi had married the Pole, Martha Hélène von Stawoski (née Teichner, 1888–1967), a glamorous beauty 10 years his junior. Their son, Hasso Conrad, was born in 1922. There were rumours that, at some point in her past, Jolly had been the mistress of a Russian prince. She had spent the war in Hollywood, where she acquired the nickname 'Jolly' (for the French *jolie* – beautiful). Uncle Willi had met her at a reception for the former German Crown Prince with her then husband, a Mr McConnell of Hollywood. Josefine disapproved of everything she stood for, but Marlene loved her. More a sister than an aunt, Jolly became a close friend; Marlene was invited frequently to raid her wardrobe. She borrowed furs, dresses, shoes and jewels, whenever she needed them. Jolly also would pass on her useful secrets to the aspiring actress; she knew how to survive with little, and appear to have much. One of her tricks was to use paste for every third diamond, giving a brilliant effect, at far less expense. Marlene always thought her one of her most beautiful and glamorous influences.

I simply wasn't ambitious, nor have I ever been . . . it was the least of my worries . . . My German upbringing helped me to cope with sudden fame . . . As the well-behaved little girl I've always tried to be, I've lived exclusively on my own talents. I've had my share of bad luck, and sometimes I've been through hell, but I've always emerged from the pits, radiant I might add.[51]

Marlene pursued her new calling indefatigably; she devoted every ounce of energy and time she had previously given to music to becoming an actress. Berthold Held was not much of a teacher, in fact, a bit of a fool, but as an administrator he kept Grete and Marlene on top of possible auditions within the Reinhardt establishment. Together, they took outdoor classes in gymnastics and English, as well as the usual Reinhardt regime of rhythmic movement, fencing, and elocution. At the Hochschule für Musik, Marlene studied singing with Dr Oskar Daniel, the best vocal coach in Berlin. He had trained for opera in Italy, but 'short, stout and bald' his stage career had been non-existent.[45] To help pay her bills, Marlene did a little modelling and had the odd job, like selling gloves. In 1921 she had her first break: She became one of the dancers who travelled with Guido Thielscher's Revue and with Rudolf Nelson's Girls.

Marlene was willing to do anything to get what she wanted. Her fantastic outfits – sometimes sheer chiffon, sometimes a monocle and a fox fur boa, paired with an almost demure appearance – got her noticed in casting calls for extras. With her astounding determination to succeed, she bussed herself around Berlin, so she might appear in three walk-on parts in three different acts, in three different plays, all in the same night. Her enthusiasm paid off. In 1922, she made it on to the playbills of three productions. These were minor parts, but she was working and gradually getting noticed. Everything was beginning to go to plan.

Marlene Dietrich's Uncle Willi with his glamorous wife, Tante Jolly

Dietrich was living in Berlin during a time many consider the 'Golden Age' of cinema. Some of the greatest 'expressionist' films were made in Weimar during the 1920s, many of which are considered to be seminal to the film canon. Prior to 1914 only about 14 per cent of the films shown in Germany were German. The war had shut the door on outside production as the focus shifted to propaganda films. By 1922, inflation was keeping international investors away; without any chance of an economic upturn, there was really no incentive to bring films into the country. During the Weimar Republic, the German film industry flourished in its own independent direction, no longer controlled by censorship, and unified in the UFA studios. This organization had been formed in 1917, by combining several smaller firms. German directors, actors, and producers, most of whom had never seen the work of the 1920s Hollywood stars such as Gloria Swanson, Rudolf Valentino, Charlie Chaplin, Douglas Fairbanks, Mary Pickford and D W Griffith, blossomed, producing a unique assortment of riches. These included several extraordinary

Marlene Dietrich worked for the chorus, as an extra and a model. Anything to bring her closer to success

talents such as Erich Pommer, Ernst Lubitsch, Fritz Lang, and eventually Dietrich herself. Their European experience enriched and energised the Hollywood film industry in the early decades of the 20th century

By 1922, Marlene believed she was perfect for the screen. She had already crossed the difficult first hurdle; she was a working actress and, slowly but surely, she was making it on to casting directors' lists. She could do the same with film; she only needed a chance to prove it. Thanks to Uncle Willi's film connections she managed to get a screen test. An executive at 'Decla' (an important film company, which would soon become part of UFA studios) assigned her to one of his cinematographers, Stefan Lorant. Lorant later recalled how, hardly keen after a full day's work shooting *Der Kampf um's Ich* (*Struggle for Myself*), he filmed her outside, jumping on and off a fence, while the crew and cast watched her energetic efforts. As far as Lorant was concerned, the test was awful. She looked unattractive and was over-enthusiastic. In his opinion, Marlene Dietrich had no future in film.

Wilhelm Dieterle was one of the actors who watched her that day. He was much more impressed than Lorant. 'Marlene never changed,' he later said. 'Many people have dreams behind them, many before them. Marlene carried hers with her always, wearing them as a halo.'[46] He liked her energy then and would remember her later. At the brink of a very successful directing career, Dieterle was already collecting actors and actresses. He was generally disillusioned with what film was achieving, and felt that directors and cinematographers frequently failed to show actors off to their best advantage.

He believed he could do much better, and was raising money to direct and act in his own script.

While Dieterle was finding the capital he needed, Marlene landed a small part in her first film, *Der kleine Napoleon* (*The Little Napoleon*, 1922). She is virtually unrecognizable in the walk-on part of a maid and is reputed to have said upon seeing herself, *I look like a potato with hair*. She was not entirely wrong. The embarrassing memory of such roles later made Dietrich want to forget that she had ever appeared in silent films.[47] Acting coy and far too cute, she comes across as untrained, and really

Marlene Dietrich's first (silent) film role as a maid in *The Little Napoleon*. She thought she looked like '*a potato with hair*'.

rather vulgar. Fortunately, the film's release was delayed, so she had not seen herself in the role by the time she accepted the part of a shopkeeper's daughter in Dieterle's *Der Mensch am Wege* (*The Man by the Roadside*, 1922). Based on a short story by Tolstoy, it was shot entirely outdoors and on a very low budget. It was not a memorable film, but she was noticed, she looked good and, more importantly, she was acting on screen. After all, that was the only thing that really mattered to her.

Then she met Rudolf Sieber, and her life took another course.

Violin: the symbol of my broken dream [48]

Berlin

RUDI 1922–1926

Dietrich was a young woman growing up in a time when anything seemed possible for women. This optimism was to shape her personality and choices ever afterwards. The liberal lifestyle, which characterized the Weimar woman, was a model for her behaviour.

Although the Nazis sought to portray the Weimar years as decadent and promiscuous, this was not wholly accurate. Despite the new liberated values, many of the traditional principles still persisted. Women might have taken on the male roles, but they still accepted, even longed for, the imposition of male authority. These contrary values would continue to define the German woman through the Nazi years. Dietrich was a product of this unlikely marriage of total liberation and traditional values. Throughout her life, she remained at once the *Hausfrau* and the temptress; pampering her man one moment, and asserting her independence the next. That anyone could get hurt in the process seemed ludicrous to her. She was not a disloyal wife, simply not a monogamous one.

Marlene met Rudolf Sieber (nicknamed Rudi) in 1922 at a casting of extras for a Joe May film, *Tragödie der Liebe* (*Tragedy of Love*, 1923) which was to star May's wife, Mia, Emil

World War I had deprived the Weimar Women of their men, the Republic gave them the vote, advances in medicine provided them with the choice when to have children. Having access to secondary education, the possibility of a career, and their own income, opened up the male world to the Weimar Women. They drove cars, flew aeroplanes, smoked in public and wore trousers and ties. Open marriages allowed both partners sexual freedom hitherto unknown. Homosexual relationships – although still illegal – were no longer hidden. The Weimar Women were forced back into their traditional roles when the Nazis took over.

Jannings and many other well-known Berlin performers. May was one of the founders of German cinema, often spoken of in the same reverent breath as Ernst Lubitsch. Sieber was his assistant, in charge of casting minor roles and hiring extras. Marlene had joined just about every other aspiring Berlin actress and wannabe in the long queues for audition, when Sieber's assistant, Fritz Maurischat singled her out. She was wearing fitted chiffon and garish green gloves. 'Aside from the attire,' Maurischat remembered, 'one could easily have overlooked her. To get my attention, the other girls were throwing breasts and legs at me, but she was demure and modest. But when she moved there was something in her movements [making me think], my God, that girl is attractive.'[49] Rudi cast her. 'She looked so ridiculous in that contrived outfit!' he later told his daughter. 'Like a child playing grown-up! I wanted to laugh. Of course, I didn't. I gave her the job. Even under all that junk, she looked right for the part of Lucie.'[50]

For her part, Marlene was swept off her feet, suddenly her career no longer mattered; she simply fell in love. Rudolf Sieber was a Czech-Austrian Catholic, born 20 February 1897 in Aussig (now Ústí nad Labem), near Prague. He was 25 years old, blonde, brown-eyed, good-looking, athletic, charming, and intelligent. Many women loved him. At the time, he was engaged to Mia May's daughter, Eva. That autumn, after Sieber and Eva May broke up on account of Marlene, Eva committed suicide by cutting her wrists. Despite Marlene having stolen her daughter's fiancé, and even indirectly having caused her death, Mia May liked Marlene. 'I remember her as very funny and engaging, attractive and original. No man could resist her. She went everywhere with a monocle and a boa of five red foxes. On other occasions, she would wear a wolf fur throw.

I loved Rudolf Sieber, not because he helped me but because he was blonde, tall and clever – everything that a young girl longs for . . . He was nice; he was gentle; he gave me the feeling that I could trust him, and this feeling was sustained during all the years of our marriage. Our trust was reciprocal and total. We were young. Such mutual faith back then was extremely rare in the decadent, cynical world of Germany in the twenties. Rudolf meant everything to me. [51]

People would follow her in the streets, they would laugh at her, but she fascinated them. She fell for Rudi right away.'[52]

The four-hour film was extensively cut for its US release, losing most of Mia May's part in the process. But Marlene made it on to the screen, in court and casino scenes, sporting her monocle and plenty of attitude. She had not yet seen herself on film and her acting shows it, but by now she was demonstrating her potential.

In Josefine's opinion, her well-brought-up daughter was meant for something better than an assistant to a film director, but Marlene had made up her mind. She was marrying Rudolf Sieber, and there was nothing that anyone could say or do to stop her. Josefine was distressed. Liesel had already married what the family called a 'low-class rotter'.[53] She had a son-in-law to whom no one ever referred. Liesel's husband, Georg Will, was a cabaret owner for the basement club of the famous (and still operating) *Theater des Western*. He had given Marlene one of her first review roles and credited himself (like so many others would) with her discovery. Even if Josefine had hoped for a better match for her beautiful Marlene, without the means to provide her with a dowry there was little she could do beyond controlling the courtship. Marlene was living at home again and Josefine quizzed Sieber regularly. He was beginning to get annoyed at having to beg, as there were plenty of other available girls with less difficult families to be had, and he told Marlene so. She was getting worried, knowing she had time to lose. Eventually Josefine accepted her choice and sent out the official announcement of their engagement on 12 November 1922.

Following Bismarck's separation of State and Church, a couple needed the official certificate, issued at the City Hall, to marry in church. On Thursday, 17 May 1923, Marlene Dietrich and Rudolf Sieber registered at Standesamt Berlin-Friedenau with Josefine von Losch (age 41) and a grocer Richard Neuhauser (age 45) – perhaps Josefine's boyfriend – as witnesses. According to Dietrich and a wedding photograph taken on what look like church steps, Rudi and Marlene were married, maybe on that same day, in her favourite church, Kaiser-Wilhelm-Gedächtnis Kirche (the Kaiser Wilhelm Memorial Church, today nicknamed the 'lipstick and the powder box' after being almost entirely destroyed by Allied bombing). He was 26 and she was 21, dressed in virginal white, with a garland of myrtle in her hair. (Marlene ripped the myrtle hairpiece in half, so that it might, at least to Sieber and the ones who knew, better represent her less-than-pure past.) The couple moved into a furnished flat in Nassauische Strasse.

Family occasions continued to be a strain for Sieber, as Josefine ensured that he was made to feel inferior at all times. His wife longed for a child but he knew they could not afford it. They were both working: Marlene at night in the theatre, Sieber on films which

Marlene Dietrich and Rudolf Sieber (1897–1976) were married on 17 May 1923 – a Thursday. The account of the actual wedding varies from a church wedding, to an unplanned visit to the registry office

necessitated occasional absences from home. At night, they would both frequent Berlin's nightspots, jazz clubs, cabarets and transvestite bars; though not always together.

In addition to the opposition from Marlene's family, Rudi was envied and pitied by his peers. Despite the growing liberal attitude within Berlin, Marlene had garnered a reputation for being promiscuous. Sometimes it would get her roles, sometimes it would lose them, but by the spring of 1924 she was credited with eleven parts on stage, and four on film.

Josefine was beginning to worry that her daughter's nomadic

lifestyle and her congenital philandering might make it impossible for her to settle down, at least not without a little help. She moved the couple to Kaiseralle 54, so she could be close at hand and ready to take on any baby-sitting duties, which she hoped were imminent.

Josefine's plan worked. By April 1924, when Marlene opened in the role as the servant girl in Molière's *Le Malade Imaginaire* (*The Imaginary Invalid*, 1924) she was two months pregnant. She took the rest of the year off, and on 13 December 1924 gave birth in hospital to her only child, Maria Elisabeth Sieber. Due to the Siebers' non-exclusive marriage, some rumoured falsely that Rudi was not the father. There was, however, no chance of any more children. Marlene had ended their physical relationship while she was pregnant. From then on the Siebers lived together in a platonic relationship, referring to each other as 'Mutti' and 'Papi'.54 They remained close friends throughout their lives and were often

mistaken for brother and sister. The arrangement did not entirely please Sieber, but now they had a child to consider, and he would not have wanted to lose either his newborn daughter or his wife in a messy divorce. Friendship was better than nothing.

Marlene enjoyed being pregnant and loved being a mother. She breast-fed for nine months to secure the health of her child, and relished the sense of power and connection it gave her with her infant. She was an excellent mother, and she made sure her efforts were acknowledged. In the years to come, she would complain

Three-year-old Maria with her mother

repeatedly to her daughter that the sacrifice of nursing had destroyed her youthful body and breasts. This was just the beginning of many destructive patterns that developed between mother and daughter, trapping Maria in a nightmarish fluctuation between appropriate guilt and appreciation. But for those first months, Marlene lived solely for her child, lavishing all of her love on her. This could not last. Berlin in 1925 was not a place or a time where artists could afford keeping a wife at home. Marlene was still only 23. She soon grew restless.

Marlene had never known a time when she or the women around her had depended on men. She was raised by a generation of women who had lost their men to war. Most of her life her mother had been single, mourning a dead husband, whilst controlling the pension and the money he left her. Love had never been a constant in the Dietrich household; it could come and be gone at a day's notice. Any love, any relationship, however awful, seemed romantic in the light of war. Alternating between these two extremes was the only way Marlene knew how to love and be loved. This confused anyone who ever cared for her. Her daughter never dared to trust her mother's love and feared its intermittent withdrawal.

In September 1925, after 18 months of pregnancy and nursing, the 'Weimar Woman' won out over the 'mother'. Marlene went back to work. The Siebers hired a young country girl, Betsy, to take care of Maria. Josefine was always ready to baby-sit, however much she disapproved of her daughter's career. In a sheer body stocking, Marlene played Eve in both parts of George Bernard Shaw's *Back to Methuselah*, one opening in November 1925, the other in January 1926. Her reviews were encouraging enough, the critics thought her excellent and 'amusing'.[55] She was back in business.

Joe May had retired from the film industry after the death of his daughter, so Sieber had taken a job as assistant to the Hungarian one-time journalist-turned-producer/director, Alexander Korda. Through Sieber, Marlene got a part in Korda's *Eine Dubarry von Heute* (*A Modern Dubarry*) starring his wife Maria Corda (from whom he had borrowed his name). The picture was an over-produced flop, but it earned Marlene a more positive mention than that given to its (none too pleased) star, Maria Corda. Marlene was slowly beginning to learn the language of film and, crucially, to translate her alluring stage persona to the screen.

By now the Siebers were sleeping in separate bedrooms; she in the master bedroom and he down the hall in his study. It was only a matter of time before Sieber found a replacement for Marlene. On another Korda/Corda picture, Sieber's friend, the future Paris celebrity photographer Alexander Choura, introduced Tamara (Tami) Matul to him. Her family name was Nikolayevna. She was a dark-eyed Russian beauty, several years younger than Marlene. She and Marlene had danced together in the chorus line and were friends. As Sieber had accepted that there was no chance of physical reconciliation with Marlene, Tami became his partner for life. Maria adored Tami, who took on the role of occasional mother, accepting the responsibility of raising her during Marlene's increasingly frequent absences.

Marlene had become a Berlin celebrity. In 1925, she landed the supporting role in Arthur Robinson's film, *Manon Lescaut* (1926). Reviews singled her out as 'the exceptionally pretty Marlene Dietrich, whom one would like to see again'.[56] But her real attention was still to the stage. In 1926, she took over Erika Glässner's role as 'Mistress of Ceremonies' in *Von Mund zu Mund* (*From Mouth to Mouth*, a revue in 18 acts, 1926) when Glässner became ill just after opening night. Marlene was a hit. Hubert ('Hubsie') von Meyerinck, a colleague from *Manon Lescaut*, remembers it as the evening that made her style. 'It was not the acting or what [she] actually did, but a certain 'nothing' which was what later made [her] famous. [She] made a style out of this 'nothing', with a look, with one breathless word, [she] said more than an accomplished comedian could with an entire scene.'[57] The cast list included the cabaret star, Claire Waldoff who many consider one of Dietrich's big influences. Waldoff's coarse and throaty voice, with its arch and comic timing had a major impact on Dietrich's style, but the inspiration went far beyond acting. Dietrich had her first physical lesbian affair with Waldoff; the experience seems to have had the effect of completing Dietrich's eroticism, both on and off the stage. There and then, she established her persona, the potent blend of male and female, which became her trademark.

VIENNA 1927–1928

After their film successes, the Korda/Corda team left for Hollywood. Sieber had taken on a rather poorly paid job as production manager for the stunt star, Harry Piel. Piel had styled himself the Douglas Fairbanks of Germany, and made popular but somewhat trashy films. Marlene was now the main breadwinner of the family and Sieber, frequently, the parent left in charge of Maria.

In the summer of 1927, Marlene left Sieber, Tami and Maria behind in Berlin to take a job in a small revue, *Wenn man zu dritt* (*Three's Company*, 1927) in Vienna. She stayed there for half a year, also taking the role of the dance girl, Rubie, in George Abbott and Philip Dunning's stage play, *Broadway* (1927), and the female lead in Gustav Ucicky's film, *Café Electric* (1927).

Emotionally, this was an important time for Dietrich. Having left her family at home, it was her first return to complete freedom after becoming a mother. Suddenly alone, she could go out all night without parental obligations. This time also established the Siebers's home setup for the years to come. Sieber, not entirely pleased by being 'the man left behind', moved Tami into the apartment; she became a permanent fixture in all of their lives.

Meanwhile, Marlene began an affair with the Austrian actor, Willi Forst (1903–80), her co-star in *Café Electric*, who would remain a lifelong friend. She was also fascinated with the film's other star, Igor Sym, a gorgeous Bavarian, who played the piano beautifully. He may well have been homosexual, their attachment platonic; this was something Dietrich never minded. She was always content to eschew sexual relationships with her admirers as long as they

Willi Forst with Dietrich in *Dangers of the Engagement Period* (1928). They became lovers in Vienna and stayed life-long friends

courted her exclusively and intensely. Sym taught her to play the Musical Saw, another of her lasting trademarks. Her years of violin practise had not been entirely wasted. Marlene had been forced to quit the violin because of tendonitis in her left hand. The Musical Saw requires a peerless right hand (bowing) technique, but the left hand's requirement is rudimentary. She was very proud of this new and difficult skill, besides, as she played with the saw between her legs, it showed them off beautifully. She would later play to entertain the American troops during World War II, allowing the illusion of exposing herself to the GI's. Ironically, at the same time Sym was executed by the Polish underground government in 1941, for his collaboration with the Gestapo.

The novel *All Quiet on the Western Front* broke the silence about World War I. Erich Maria Remarque's unprecedented and immediate worldwide bestseller (describing a soldier's experience in WWI) echoed the disillusion of many: the war seemed absurd in retrospect. The reactions to the book showed up the divides in the Weimar Republic. The liberals accepted its thesis, the conservatives thought the war had been unpleasant but necessary. The fascists found the book a slur on anybody who had fought in the war. They used the war and the 'Dolchstoss Legende' (the legend that the German Army had been not defeated but stabbed in the back) most effectively in their propaganda.[58]

During dinners and lunches, Willi Forst introduced her to the Vienna 'in-crowd', including Billy Wilder (1906–2002), who was then still just a journalist; he would later direct her in some of her best roles. She also met Hans von Twardovski and Erich Maria Remarque, soon to be world famous for his epochal war novel, *All Quiet on the Westen Front* (1928), and her lover 15 years later. She was often seen with Leonhard Frank and the historical novelist Heinrich Mann, along with the great comedian Max Pallenberg and his wife, the singer

Fritzi Massary. 'She could easily hold her own,' Massary said of Dietrich later. 'She had the greatest capacity a person can have: she could laugh at herself. [She easily] could hold her own in our circle.'[59] Dietrich loved a good conversation, and always preferred the thinking and intelligent artist for long-term friendships, dinner dates and entertainment. Beauty was of value for passing flings only, if at all.

ALMOST FAMOUS 1928–1929

In the early spring of 1928, Marlene brought Willi Forst and her role as Rubie back to Berlin, where 'Broadway' opened, under different direction on 9 March 1928. Although she had starred as Rubie in Vienna, that did not ensure her the role in the Berlin staging of 'Broadway'. Every dancer had wanted the part and it was an honour in itself to have been offered it.

As a result of Vienna's culinary pleasures Marlene had gained weight and was now the heaviest she had been since before her pregnancy. She started to exercise vigorously. Every morning she boxed with a professional trainer, a Turk named Sabri Mahia. She even discussed with him her daughter's supposedly crooked legs. Having discovered Maria's weakness upon her return from Vienna she was frightened that her daughter might become disabled and was unconvinced that exercise could cure this problem. As was common at the time, Maria legs were put into metal braces every night until she was seven years old.

Although home, Marlene did not take on the responsibilities of mother and *Hausfrau*. (Later, Dietrich loved her role as provider within the home: she would cook and clean for her family, lovers, and sick employees and even when she stayed for weekends with friends.) In 1928, she was too busy to cook, so her mother would often come by to drop off dishes for the many dinner parties the Siebers were now hosting. Tami, conveniently, was there to look after Maria.

Friends and acquaintances remember that, during this time,

Dietrich was carefree but ambitious, and that she constantly carried around a newly acquired portable gramophone player. It was as if she was suddenly missing music, and the importance it had once had in her life, and for her career. She listened longingly to anything from Ravel and Debussy, to Irving Berlin and Whisperin' Jack Smith. Jazz and American songs were at the height of their popularity in Europe, and Marlene, as always, outdid all other fans in her obsessive enthusiasms.

She was becoming a style herself without realizing it. Her reputation grew by simply being 'Marlene Dietrich'. Even if her film reviews were mixed, she was getting good roles in cabaret and ever wider recognition. However, she was still limited to relatively minor roles, playing coquettes and demi-mondaines. Producers and directors did not trust her abilities enough to offer her serious parts on stage or the leads in A-movies. Marlene herself believed that it was only a matter of time before this happened. As she told anyone who wanted to listen, including Felix Jackson, production assistant on 'Broadway', *I shall be a very big star, very soon.*[60]

That same spring she began rehearsals for a Marcellus Schiffer/ Mischa Spoliansky revue (in 24 scenes) called *Es liegt in der Luft – ein Spiel in Warenhaus* (*It's in the Air – a play in a department store*, 1928). Berlin celebrities, Margo Lion, a French cabaret star, and her husband Marcellus Schiffer adored Marlene. Schiffer was at the height of his fame, having shocked Paris with his immoral fairytale – the good turned wicked, the wicked turned good – Berlin loved him. *Es liegt in der Luft* was a satire on modern Germany. Set in an elegant Berlin department store, it follows a pair of twins, lost by their parents on a shopping trip. Abandoned, they are raised in secrecy by the shop staff, and never leave the store, even as adults. Decades later, their parents come back to find them, but the twins have grown up, with children and grandchildren of their own. As if nothing in the world had changed, their parents cannot accept their children might have grown up, and mistake their great-grandchildren for the lost twins. The cast, headed by Oskar Karlweiss, Margo Lion, and

We were going to sing a duet called 'My Best Girlfriend', Margo was to sing high and I was to sing low. I fastened big bunches of violets to both our shoulders to give our outfits, which I found a bit too mournful, a friendly touch of colour. Little did I know that violets in the Berlin theatrical world of the twenties had taken on a rather special meaning. I was flabbergasted when I read the review describing 'an androgynous song' as the high point of the performance and heightened by the violets on our shoulders. I didn't dare ask Margo Lion to explain it all to me. She probably would have laughed at my gaucherie and naïveté. 'Androgynous!' I had no idea what the critic meant.[61]

Marlene was a smash hit overnight. Now even closer to fame, Marlene Dietrich's name was on everyone's lips.

Tami danced in the show as a chorus girl. Sieber paced the

wings watching both of his women acting the jealous husband, whilst flaunting his affair. This was the last time they performed together.

Marlene sang several of the popular songs from the show. One duo with Hans Carl Müller celebrated the sexual thrill of stealing. Another, the notorious, 'Wenn meine beste Freundin' / 'When my special girlfriend', would always be remembered as one of her defining moments.

This song is very specifically about a lesbian relationship between two friends. It made even the hardened Berliner audiences sit up and notice her, giving her five curtain calls mid-show. Marlene had pinned violets (the 'secret' sign for homosexuality) on her and Margo's dresses to drive the point home. It did. Marlene was notorious overnight. The play had 140 performances and the songs from the show were recorded in June 1928, the first recording of Dietrich. After the show, her name – and her legs – were everywhere. Etam artificial silk stockings used her legs to publicize their product on playbills. She now happily allowed her legs to take on an almost mythical nature of their own. Years later she permitted rumours to circulate that the legs had been insured at Lloyd's of London for a million marks. They were not, but who was to contradict her, or even care? The story was too good not to be true.

Marlene had found her style and Berlin had caught on to it as well. Immediately after *Es liegt in der Luft* she was cast, very successfully, in George Bernard Shaw's *Parents and Children* (1928) as the spoiled daughter, Hypatia Tarleton. By now she possessed all the arrogance that Shaw could have wished for in the part. A friend from the cast, Lili Darvas, interviewed in the 1970s said, 'Marlene already had extraordinary equipment when I worked with her. She had the rarest capacity of all, the capacity to be completely still on the stage and yet to command the absolute attention of an audience . . . Marlene would sit downstage smoking a cigarette very slowly and sexily, and people forgot the rest of us were around. She had such natural grace, there was so much melody in her voice, she had such economy of gesture . . . She had the one essential star quality: she could be magnificent doing nothing.'[62] Audiences enjoyed her, even if the critics were still slightly bemused. The reviews were unable to look much beyond her legs, and few saw any talent beyond her sex appeal. 'If she showed less, that in itself would have been enough,' one critic wrote. Another was even less enthusiastic: 'The eloquence of her legs was not able to replace her lack of talent.'[63] A disastrous appearance in *Das Schiff der verlorenen Menschen* (*The Ship of Lost Men*, 1929) could quite possibly have destroyed her career, had she not received good reviews for her two previous films, *Die Frau, nach der man sich sehnt* (*The Woman One Longs For* also known as *Three Loves*, 1929) and *Ich küsse Ihre Hand, Madame* (*I Kiss Your Hand, Madame*, 1929).

Audiences were beginning to recognize her, but her director, Kurt (later Curtis) Bernhardt, who had fought to use her in *Die Frau, nach der man sich sehnt* (1929), found her to be a complete nuisance. By then, Marlene had studied her screen image and done private photo shoots. She knew now how to avoid her potato-look. Convinced her nose was unattractive and that her chin was weak, she decided that she looked good only in frontal shots. 'She was a real bitch,'[64] Bernhardt said later. 'For a thousand roubles she wouldn't move her bloody face! I got pretty impatient with her!'[65] Her co-star, Fritz Kortner, completely smitten, defended her, which only caused Bernhardt to fight with her all the more. His comments were so irrationally critical. even years after he directed her. that they might be interpreted as jealousy. Apparently Marlene did not readily sleep with everyone on her path to fame; unhappily for him, Bernhardt did not make the list.

There are claims from an ex-lover that, around this time, Dietrich had cosmetic surgery. Later, rumours claimed that she had her molars removed to emphasize her cheekbones. Although Dietrich might have taken to such drastic measures, however expensive and modern they were at the time, there seems no other evidence, visual or otherwise, to support this. It was always vigorously denied by Dietrich, who used lighting and, later, typical theatrical facelifts (using tape under a wig) to give her face the 'Dietrich-look'. Successful acting, a well-placed light, make-up and a manipulated photograph will always be far more effective than surgery.

In *Ich küsse Ihre Hand, Madame,* despite her full figure and the slightly uninteresting role as a rich divorcée (who falls for an ex-Russian Count now a waiter), Marlene was sensually beautiful. She not only captivated the audience with dramatic skill but she 'ate the lens'. Her newly acquired visual control of her image had worked wonders, and was showing its effect. Suddenly film reviewers were comparing her to Greta Garbo and she was hailed as the German promise of a rival to the Hollywood star.

Years later, another false rumour circulated, which credited Marlene with having been an extra in Garbo's (only) German film, an Asta Nielsen vehicle, *Die freudlose Gasse* (*The Joyless Street*) (1925). Dietrich was confused with the German actress, Hertha von Walter, who always insisted she played the supposed Dietrich part. At the time of the shoot, Marlene was at home nursing her two-and-a-half-month-old daughter Maria. Dietrich greatly admired Garbo and would have welcomed the rumour that she had rubbed shoulders with her before she herself was a star.

Dietrich's principle that a white lie is only a real lie if you are found out, served her well throughout her life. From early on, Dietrich understood that to be a star and eventually a legend, certain special stories are essential. A star must give their audiences the sense that they know him or her intimately, the feeling that they have heard the star's most secret truths. Only a fool would give away anything real, as it would pale into insignificance compared to the fantasies people have imagined in its absence.

Sex. In America an obsession.
In other parts of the world a fact.[66]

The Blue Angel

JOSEF VON STERNBERG 1929–1930

On 16 August 1929, Josef von Sternberg and his wife, Riza Royce, an English actress, arrived by train in Berlin. His wife had accompanied him on the journey from Hollywood in an effort to revive their troubled marriage. He had been invited to the UFA studios with Erich Pommer, Germany's greatest producer, to direct a film starring Emil Jannings. This was to be Germany's first talking picture, and had a budget of $325,000.

Pommer was certain that a talking picture with Jannings in the lead would fix German cinema on the international map. He also needed something successful to re-establish himself at UFA studios, as he had been fired in 1927 due to the high cost of *Metropolis,* which he produced. Since then he had been working in Hollywood; his connection with both worlds could make him a useful player for the UFA executives. Jannings had won the first acting Academy

Josef von Sternberg (Jonas Sternberg) (1894–1969) Austrian-American director was born in Vienna to Orthodox Jewish parents. In 1908, his family moved to the US permanently. After the war, he worked his way up through production to film director. He was a great pictorial stylist and brought a new perspective to the art of film-maker. An egocentric and tyrannical visionary, he had as many failures as critical and commercial hits, causing him to be called both a genius and a menace to the film business by Hollywood. Known once as the man who began the gangster genre, his name is now inextricably linked to Dietrich. He is supposed to have said: 'The only way to succeed is to make people hate you, that way they remember you.' He never regained his career post-Dietrich, but before his death in 1969, critics finally reclaimed him as the true genius he was. Dietrich and von Sternberg kept in touch to the end of his life.

Josef von Sternberg and Marlene Dietrich during the filming of
The Blue Angel. Dietrich created her own costumes, her original sense
of style adding to the part

Award (1928) in Hollywood for his role as a Russian general in von
Sternberg's *The Last Command* (1927), but had returned to Germany
as American film embraced sound. His command of English was,
to say the least, uncertain. Pommer knew that he needed a bilingual
director to help Jannings's English in the German and English versions of the film. He had hoped to lure Ernst Lubitsch back from
Paramount, but Lubitsch's demand for $60,000 was way beyond
his means.

The Austrian-born Josef von Sternberg was also a Paramount
Pictures director and German/English speaking. However, immediately after *The Last Command* he had vowed never to work with
Jannings again, not even 'if he was the last remaining actor on
Earth'.[67] But now he needed money. Jannings had specifically written
asking von Sternberg to direct the picture and the latter had eventually agreed for the sum of $40,000. (Jannings was to be paid $50,000
plus an extra $25,000 if the film were to be released in the USA.)

The new Jannings/von Sternberg project was supposed to be an adaptation of the life of Rasputin but upon arrival in Berlin von Sternberg refused even to consider this. To the complete surprise of Pommer and Jannings, he told the press that he was still looking for the right material. As the legal problems associated with *Rasputin* multiplied, Pommer pushed for an adaptation of the novel by Heinrich Mann, *Professor Unrat* (*End of a Tyrant*). Jannings and Pommer had already discussed the book the summer before, though they avoided telling von Sternberg this. He felt it yielded promising possibilities, and they all liked the idea of a respectable high-school professor falling for a dubious cabaret star. Supervising the script, von Sternberg rewrote the story to be less about the professor and more about the dancing girl, Lola Lola. He named the film after Lola Lola's cabaret, *Der Blaue Engel* (*The Blue Angel*, 1929). It worked well; 'blau' and 'blue' were slang in both English and German for 'drunk' and 'depressed' and would mirror the professor's intoxication with Lola Lola. Now all von Sternberg needed was an actress who could be addictive enough for a man to sacrifice everything for her love.

Marlene was far from being the first choice for Lola Lola; at the outset she was not even considered. Practically every hopeful actress in Berlin was paraded before von Sternberg: he rejected them all, including Marlene. But he would not proceed with the film without casting what he considered to be the right actress. Whenever the studio pushed him to make his decision, he threatened to give up and return to Hollywood. Every actress in Berlin knew he was looking, and every actress also knew she had been refused, Marlene included.

As von Sternberg's search continued in vain, his friend, Leni Riefenstahl (1902–), ex-dancer, actress and soon-to-be director, began to covet the part of Lola Lola herself, although she never auditioned. Her impressions of that time were recalled many years after the war. They are full of ambiguities and, perhaps, intentional manipulations of the truth – Riefenstahl and Marlene may have moved in the same circles, but they were hardly close acquaintances.

Nevertheless Riefenstahl is alleged to have said to von Sternberg: 'Marlene Dietrich? I've seen her only once, but I was struck by her. She was in a small artists' cafe on Rankestrasse with some young actresses, and my attention was drawn by her deep, throaty voice . . . Very sexy, but a bit common. Maybe she was a little tipsy. I heard her say quite loudly, "Why must we always have beautiful bosoms? Why can't they droop a little?" Upon which she lifted up her left breast and amused herself with it, startling the young girls sitting around her. Yes, she might be a good type for you.'[63]

Although Riefenstahl appears rational and in favour of Dietrich, there is an undertone of jealousy and disapproval, as if she had been von Sternberg's preferred Berliner sweetheart until Dietrich came along. The common opinion, which Riefenstahl shared, was that, even if von Sternberg was looking for someone sluttish to play Lola Lola, Marlene was much too louche, even for him.

In 1929, Marlene had just lost the lead in *Pandora's Box* to Louise Brooks, a former Ziegfield girl. She had absolutely no reason to believe that UFA studios would cast her in their first sound film. Regardless of her inability to land anything but leads in mediocre B-films, Marlene was enjoying public and critical

Leni Riefenstahl was an extraordinary artist, but here role as director under Hitler has always been cause of much controversy, putting into question everything she said and produced before and since World War II. When in 1991, Dietrich received a letter asking her to 'clear up a few things, which to the great regret of Leni Riefenstahl, might be standing between her and you', Dietrich wrote 'Nazi' on the back and did not respond. Of course, by this time Dietrich was calling everyone of whom she disapproved 'Nazi', and she had long locked herself away, no longer going out or receiving visitors.[59]

acclaim on the stage in *Zwei Krawatten* (*Two Bow Ties*, 1929). Mischa Spoliansky (the show's composer and the composer from *Es liegt in der Luft*) had recommended her for the role of Mabel in this satirical revue in nine scenes; it proved to be a perfect vehicle for Marlene. A gangster pays a waiter, Jean (Hans Albers), a lottery ticket and 1,000 marks to swap ties with him (a waiter's black with a gentleman's white) and thereby help him escape the police. The lottery ticket wins Jean a first-class trip on a steamer where he meets Mabel (Dietrich). After much flirtation on the boat, watched by Jean's fiancée Trude, Mabel and Jean get engaged. The story ends on a conservatively moral note. After a trip to Chicago to meet Mabel's rich aunt, Mrs Robinson (Rosa Valetti – Marlene's contact to the Max Reinhardt theatre school), Jean leaves Mabel for Trude, who has unexpectedly inherited $10 million. Leaving high society behind, he stays within his own class where he belongs. Marlene's performance was a sensation. She was showered with a barrage of rave reviews.

One night in September, Josef von Sternberg went to see *Zwei Krawatten*, not for Marlene, but to observe Hans Albers and Rosa Valetti, already cast in supporting roles in his film. By this time every woman in his circle, from Pommer's wife, Gertrude, to Ruth Landshoff, Marlene's colleague from Vienna and mistress to von Sternberg's friend and his producer, Dr Karl Vollmoeller, had changed their tune and were championing her. Von Sternberg was uncompromising; the photographs he had seen were raw and unflattering, showing Marlene as an *ingénue*. Furthermore, he knew that she was also a wife and a mother, hardly what he had in mind for his 'Blue Angel'.

Marlene had been forewarned by her supporters that von Sternberg was coming to the theatre that night. Even if von Sternberg was not aware of it himself, he was coming to see *her* – that was how they had arranged it, and this fitted perfectly with her plans. Von Sternberg watched enough of the play to hear her say one line in English – perfect English. He had found 'his angel', but told no one. Von Sternberg never played by anyone's rules. He not only left the play at the interval, but also did not go backstage, breaking the rigid etiquette between acting colleagues. Although Marlene subsequently received a request to audition, she could hardly have supposed that he was interested. He had even called her 'an untalented cow' when pursued by his eager employers to give an opinion of her performance. In this way he made sure that no one else could claim to have forced the final decision on him.[70]

In the years to come, both Dietrich and von Sternberg would insist that, when they met, Marlene was a student barely out of the Max Reinhardt Drama School, that her role in the play had been minor, and that she had only had that one line in the play, that the single line in English made all the difference for von Sternberg. With this lie, Dietrich seemed younger than her 28 years and von Sternberg's discovery all the greater. In fact that fateful evening in September 1929, Marlene had eight years of acting experience behind her, more than 25 stage parts and at least 17 film roles, many of them leads. If anyone had trained Marlene Dietrich for stardom, it was Marlene herself.

Marlene knew that by all accounts, von Sternberg did not want her. He had offended her, so why should she make an effort? Besides this, Sieber had suggested that she act aloof. Not trying for the part would make her stand out from every other girl von Sternberg had auditioned. Sieber suggested that she not wear one of her 'whore outfits' but dress like a lady in her best suit, with white kid gloves and a fox fur.[71]

She met Pommer, Jannings and von Sternberg, who had her walk about the room, looking her up and down. Marlene was furious. They might be casting for Germany's first sound film, but she was a star in a Berlin hit show. She did not need another humiliating casting session, and she was really not interested in another role as a whore or demi-mondaine. After all, she was promoting herself as a serious actress. Although von Sternberg apologised for making her parade up and down, Marlene was so annoyed that she petulantly lied that she had only made three films, photographed terribly, and always received bad reviews. He knew this was untrue, and was fascinated. No one he had ever cast had invented failures in this manner before. Although he might not have known the extent of her resumé, he would have heard about her roles from mutual contacts. He knew she had appeared in at least nine films and had probably seen some of them. Regardless of her aggressively arrogant behaviour, von Sternberg invited her to take the screen test. This was an unnecessary formality, as he needed no further convincing. He cast Dietrich despite the producers and Jannings thinking her too stolid, too casual, and lacking the allure that the film needed. A further concern was that they had already decided on Lucie Mannheim. (Mannheim was a younger actress who acted with Marlene in *Duel on the Lido* and was a favourite of Jannings. He preferred plumper actresses and in this respect, Mannheim was better equipped than Marlene.) Mannheim's screen test was already scheduled and she gave a tolerable performance with Friedrich Hollaender at the piano. Von Sternberg rejected her, but kept the pianist on the film as composer.

Rumours were rife – Mannheim was the winner. However much Marlene had admired von Sternberg on their first meeting, she was sure that she would not be cast in the lead role. They might even insult her by offering one of the minor roles. Unwilling to waste her time, Marlene came to the *Blue Angel* screen test without a pre-pared song, sheet music, or a piano player. The more she resisted, the more von Sternberg was intrigued. He believed he was seeing what no one had seen before or, more importantly, what no one had truly had the nerve to cultivate. He believed that he alone could turn this actress into a star. He pinned the wardrobe-supplied dress to fit her body, told the hairdresser what to do with her hair, found her a piano player (probably the assistant to Friedrich Hollaender, Peter Kreuder), and told her to sing something she liked in English. She had been in training with her portable gramophone for months. In close-up, smoking and flirting arrogantly, she sang him the very popular, 'You're the Cream in My Coffee'. Jumping off the piano, she swore at the pianist in Berliner slang, before continuing to sing, this time in German, 'Wenn man auseinander geht!' Von Sternberg could hardly contain himself. Her perform-ance was irresistible. This was what he had been searching for in his Lola Lola, insouciance, impatience, arrogance and anger, together

'I am credited with [Marlene Dietrich's] discovery. This is not so . . . I am a teacher who took a beautiful woman, instructed her, presented her carefully, edited her charms, disguised her imperfections and led her to crystallize a pictorial aphrodisiac. She was a perfect medium, who with intelligence absorbed my direction, and despite her own misgivings responded to my conception of a female archetype.'

JOSEF VON STERNBERG [72]

with suave sexuality, and that was what he filmed. Marlene told him, that despite liking his work, she did not think that he 'handled women very well'.[73] Yet she had responded with ease to his direction, beyond anything he had previously encountered. He was determined to cast her and fought everyone at UFA studios to get his way; she was given a $5,000 contract. She ordered champagne and blew her whole fee on a mink coat. Then she began to worry. What would her mother say to her playing yet another whore? Josefine was baby-sitting Maria and she had never considered acting to be decent work, so what would she think of this role? What would all of Berlin say? What if von Sternberg suddenly wanted to film her naked? How could she show her face again after playing such a part? She might never get another serious acting job in Berlin.

DER BLAUE ENGEL

Sieber negotiated and signed Marlene's *Blue Angel* contract. When she was in need of advice, he was the last to offer it, but inevitably his was the counsel she followed. Confronted with a dilemma, she would consult Sieber and he would quietly take charge. It had always been so, and would continue, even after the arrival of von Sternberg and Dietrich's later departure for Hollywood. She might no longer share his bed, but he knew her every secret: who her lovers were, her fears, and the problems she faced. He was always there to help.

Casting was complete, so the preparations could begin. The sets were created and every shot planned, all closely supervised by von Sternberg. Hollaender had started writing the songs even

Dietrich's Lola Lola on stage with the orchestra and Friedrich Hollaender at the piano. Hollaender and Dietrich worked together repeatedly throughout her career

before the script was finished. He now wrote for Dietrich's dark, low voice, as opposed to Mannheim's lighter soprano. He was assisted by Peter Kreuder and Franz Wachsman. The songs and his music are essential parts of *The Blue Angel*, and to make the point, von Sternberg included shots of Hollaender's jazz band playing live on stage throughout.

Marlene was content to accept von Sternberg's expertise in everything, until the wardrobe department displayed the designs for Lola Lola. She was livid. What she was shown was too vulgar and predictable. Somehow, her director needed to be persuaded to let her choose the costumes instead. Over dinner, Sieber arranged

Friedrich Hollaender (1892–1976) German songwriter was born in London but grew up in Berlin where he studied music; he emigrated to the USA in 1934. He wrote songs and revues for Max Reinhardt in the 1920s and songs for more than 150 films from 1929 on, his most famous for Dietrich.

Franz Waxman (Wachsman) (1906–67) was born in Germany to Jewish parents. Hollaender hired him to arrange and conduct the score for *The Blue Angel*. In 1934 he fled to Hollywood. He won Oscars for Billy Wilder's *Sunset Boulevard* and George Steven's *A Place in the Sun*.

Marlene Dietrich during a break on *The Blue Angel*. During lunch she re-touched her make-up and hair while serving her director his meal

with von Sternberg (who most nights was dining with Marlene alone or at the Siebers') to put Dietrich in charge of her own costume.

This was what Marlene had longed for, a collaboration with someone who understood her and respected her opinions. She needed a counterpart who was just as interested as she, not only that she should look right for the role but that she be stunning as an actress. She combed the streets and transvestite bars to copy the look, and sometimes even borrow the clothes, from Berlin's prostitutes. She rummaged through her hoard of stored-away treasures, mainly stolen from previous productions. Combining lingerie, a white collar, and the famous top hat, she came up with the perfect look for Lola Lola. Von Sternberg provided the rest.

From then on, von Sternberg and Dietrich were a team, each in charge of different parts of the creation that was to become 'Marlene Dietrich'. For their first few films, von Sternberg could do no wrong in Marlene's eyes. She obeyed his every instruction, sat at his feet and took in everything he could teach her. Each day they lunched together in her dressing room as she indulged him. He was, of course, already her lover. In return, she was invited to the evening screenings of the daily rushes, and allowed to sit in on the editing as he included her in the whole process of film-making. She would eventually know as much about film-making as von Sternberg and almost any other director.

The shooting of *Der Blaue Engel* and *The Blue Angel* started on 4 November 1929 and lasted until 22 January 1930. The films were shot in sequence, the English version following the German. The actors found the English dialogue difficult, so additional shooting was completed in May, after the final edit of the film. Initially, von Sternberg had assured Marlene that she need not to worry about the English version; his wife would dub it for her. Marlene was shocked that he doubted her abilities and was determined to speak the part herself. In the English version, the language never interfered with Dietrich's acting and when she stumbled over the 'th' in 'moths', von Sternberg added sound effects to cover up her Germanic lisping. The film was scripted for the German version and several of the jokes simply disappear or do not work in translation. Dietrich's performance is exact and powerful in German, despite her supposed embarrassment at having to use Berliner slang in front of the crew. Speaking in her mother-tongue, she was Josefine von Losch's little girl, Leni, but in English, she was acting out a part. This early detachment from her bourgeois roots made the transformation into 'Marlene Dietrich' – a unique and solitary figure, belonging to nowhere and to no one – even more convincing.

The German version of *Der Blaue Engel* is an extraordinary piece of work. The English, *The Blue Angel,* a little less so, but compelling nonetheless. In both films, Dietrich acts with such total energy and ease that even today her performances are still endearingly naughty and shocking.

Almost unnoticed by Jannings and the producers, von Sternberg had managed to change the focus of the film, not only onto his own story, but also onto Lola Lola and Dietrich. Instead of being cynical, like the novel, the film is romantically fatalistic. In the film, Lola Lola is younger and without a child, and the professor does not end up in prison for corrupting the middle classes with gambling (punished with respectability for reforming the disreputable); but instead he fails both the righteous and the disgraced of society. When, against his better judgment, the professor falls for Lola Lola, he believes, despite many warnings to the contrary, that somehow marriage will make their union honourable and pure. But they are unable to live as model citizens in a good society and Lola Lola is unable to hide her shameful past behind white bridal veils. The only option for them is to live in the underworld, travelling from place to place. The professor ends up as a clown, selling his wife's image on postcards to her clients, and not doing this very successfully. A husband could hardly fall lower. When he fails to earn any money off the trade, he ironically declaims, in resignation and despair, 'Oh yes, we make a living!' To which she retorts, 'If you don't like it, you can go.'

What makes the story remarkable and modern even now, more than seventy years after it was made, is that despite the professor's failure to 'save' his wife, Lola Lola is not destroyed as he is, but walks away, triumphant. Dietrich's interpretation of the role is uncompromising; Lola Lola never apologises for being who she is, and since she never lived in the respectable world, can hold the illusion of being an artist. She is free because she never accepts her behaviour as wrong, therefore, neither does the audience. They only see her flirting with men's desires, but never actually physically entertaining them; it is as if nothing happens except in their imaginations. Lola Lola remains pure while her clients, the professor, and the audience are the ones compromised, because they accept the superficial image and wish her to prostitute herself. When the professor finally goes back to his old classroom desk to die, he has failed because he knew only how to condemn and not, like Lola Lola, how to live. She sings on happily, carefree, a new man on her arm, and one step further on her journey through life.

At first sight, the story might not seem particularly to favour the woman, but, in the hands of von Sternberg and Dietrich, Lola Lola is empowered. Like Dietrich, she can have whichever man whenever she desires him; he makes her neither respectable nor disreputable, because she is already complete as she is, she is the ultimate 'Weimar Woman'.

It is in the songs, when von Sternberg simply lets the cameras roll and allows Marlene to be all Dietrich, that the film glows. Singing Dietrich entraps and seduces anybody she chooses, be they man or woman. Hollaender's words say it all, written as if he is describing the Marlene of that time as well as the Dietrich she was to become.

Midway through shooting, Jannings realized that, regardless of his star fee, he was being upstaged. He would complain to von Sternberg, and demanded to be driven harder, allegedly asking to be whipped in his dressing room, in an attempt to improve his performance. It was to no avail, he was losing his professional standing to a newcomer. Jannings

Falling in Love Again

An enigmatic glimmer
A je-ne-sais-pas quoi
Shines always in the glance
Of a pretty woman

But when my eyes look deeply
At my vis-a-vis
And gaze intensely at him
What does it mean?

Love's always been my game
Play it how I may
I was made that way
I can't help it

Men cluster to me
Like moths around a flame
And if their wings burn
I know I'm not to blame

I often stop and wonder
Why I appeal to men
How many times I blunder
In love and out again

They offer me devotion
I like it I confess
When I reflect emotion
There's no need to get

Falling in love again
Never wanted to
What am I to do
I can't help it

stiff comic style, which was so necessary in the silent movie genre, was rapidly becoming passé. Dietrich's ease, her stillness, which had made her less than engaging on the silent screen, was exactly what talking pictures demanded. Jannings' frustration and resentment of her impending success became so great that in the fight scene between Lola Lola and the professor he almost strangled her and had to be pulled away. Her neck bruised, she felt no sympathy

Emil Jannings (1882–1952), with von Sternberg. As a supporter of the Third Reich Jannings was blacklisted after the war and died bitter and unemployed

for him. He later credited himself with her discovery and she never stopped hating him.

Von Sternberg demanded that everything should be perfect. His tyrannical perfectionism would later be notorious in Hollywood. He drove his cast and crew till he achieved his vision, doing dozens of takes, sometimes keeping everyone on set 20 hours a day. Dietrich was the perfect student; the harder he worked her, the more she loved and admired him. For her, his energy and devotion were simply an invitation to work harder.

Von Sternberg knew he had a hit on his hands and he made sure Paramount Pictures learnt of it, too. A representative from Paramount Berlin visited the set and was impressed by Dietrich's screen test. As Joseph Pasternak from Universal (with whom Dietrich would later work on *Destry Rides Again*) was interested too. Paramount Pictures would have to act fast if they did not want to lose a nascent star.

On 29 January 1930, B P Schuleberg, vice-president of Paramount Pictures, sent a telegram. This was effectively a contract, not offering, but congratulating Dietrich on joining Paramount for a seven-year contract with a weekly salary of $500, increasing to $3,000 by the end of the seventh year. Not only was Dietrich offended by the assumption that she was available for their taking, but she was scared. What if they were all mistaken and she was no good? She might have been offered a contract but that was no guarantee of success; many others had been lured to Hollywood, only to return with their careers scarred by their very public failure. Besides, she was not free to sign with anyone: UFA Studios had the right to exercise their option on her after they had screened the film, and they were still considering her. In the end they turned her down. Von Sternberg had been right; the executives of the German film industry did not recognize her talents and let her go. They could see nothing remarkable in Dietrich playing yet another lowlife role in *The Blue Angel*. Dietrich was demoralized by their response. How could she leave everything and everyone she knew for a career which, despite what von Sternberg might say, was sure to be a flop?

After 24 January 1930, UFA Studios, who had von Sternberg on loan, were paying weekly penalty payments to Paramount for keeping him in Germany. The budget of the film had soared to 2 million marks, the highest Pommer had reached to date, so UFA Studios needed to cut expenditure wherever possible. The film was complete, they did not need von Sternberg to approve the edits, or oversee the English re-shoot, so he was free to return to the USA. With Dietrich's future undecided, von Sternberg stayed for the press ball at the end of January, then left for California two days later. According to Leni Riefenstahl, she, not Dietrich, was to have been his partner for the ball. A jealous Dietrich had had a tantrum and changed the arrangements (or so von Sternberg told Riefenstahl, begging her to forgive him for changing his mind). He left Riefenstahl with promises of making her a star in Hollywood, but quickly forgot about her. Dietrich was already his star, he had no need for another.

Sieber finally made up Dietrich's mind; she had to go to the USA. Von Sternberg would be there to take care of her, so naturally she could leave her family and Berlin behind for this 'once-in-a-life-time opportunity'. [74] Back at Paramount Pictures, von Sternberg had already renegotiated her new, two-picture contract guaranteeing her $1,750 a week, with a choice of her own director, unheard of for an untried talent. She was free to return to Germany at the end of the two-picture deal but not to sign with another American studio. She accepted.

Whilst Dietrich was recording the songs from *The Blue Angel,* packing, and already missing Maria, Pommer had to deal with a disaster. UFA Studios did not understand the ending of the film. Was the professor dead? Was he alive? What was the meaning of von Sternberg's silent ending? It had to be made clear. Lacking a director the executive producers could not re-shoot. Music, it was decided, would provide the answer. They added Beethoven as the camera pulls away from Jannings, slumped over his desk. This was, in their opinion more appropriate for the emotion of death, than silence. In the re-edited versions available today, the camera pulls back when the church bells ring with the melody of the 'Bird Catcher's Song' from Mozart's *Magic Flute.* These pealing bells are exactly the right kind of ending this remarkable film demands. It could hardly be made any clearer, the professor is dead.

Der Blaue Engel was screened three times on 1 April 1930 at a huge gala evening at the Gloria-Palast, Berlin. At the last two screenings, it was arranged that the minor actors would take bows with the star of the film, Emil Jannings. Dietrich, came on stage in white chiffon and a full-length white ermine coat, the complete antithesis of Lola Lola. She was very much a star. Immediately after the show, clasping her bouquet of roses and the applause still ringing in her ears, she boarded the boat train for Bremerhaven, to catch the SS *Bremen,* setting sail for the United States the following day. Willi Forst accompanied her to the dock; Dietrich had sent Sieber home to look after Maria, who was ill with a cold and needed the consolation of at least one of her parents. A large crowd of reporters saw Dietrich off at the station – giving her a taste of what was to come in America.

As *The Blue Angel* took Europe by storm, Paramount Pictures began negotiating a deal for the rights with UFA Studios. However, they would hold back its US release until 5 December 1930, when it screened at the Rialto, New York, deliberately postponed till after the première of *Morocco,* Dietrich's first American film. They were certainly not prepared to give the UFA Studios the credit of her discovery. Paramount Pictures wanted Dietrich on the lot, on their payroll, and under their control, before she was introduced to the American audience.

Dietrich and von Sternberg were a reality. Their partnership would produce some of the most intriguing and beautiful films in both of their careers, but with ominous consequences for their personal relationship. She had become his muse, his Eve, his Galatea. She had made him her unquestioned hero, her God, her Pygmalion. Nobody can survive on such a pedestal, without ultimately disappointing the one who put them there. Dietrich and von Sternberg nearly destroyed each other in their quest for perfection.

Emil Jannings and Marlene Dietrich at the premier of *The Blue Angel* on 1 April 1930 at the Gloria-Palast, Berlin. That night Dietrich, still in evening dress, boarded the train for SS *Bremen* to sail for New York the next day

That night, only hours from leaving Berlin, Dietrich did not know what to expect. She was not yet a star, and was regretting the trip before it had even begun. Had history and circumstances not intervened, she might have returned after fulfilling her two-picture contract, satisfied with having had a lucrative year. This was not to be. Dietrich would never live in Germany again, or become a serious stage actress.

*Josef von Sternberg, the man I most
wanted to please.*[75]

Master and Pupil

Dietrich had seven days alone before reaching New York City; another week would bring her to Los Angeles. Sieber had insisted that she bring Resi, her dresser from *The Blue Angel*, for support and company on the trip and in Hollywood. Unfortunately, the weather on the crossing was so bad that, in the servants' quarters below deck, every maid, including Resi, was seasick. Resi, hanging over the rail, lost her first meal and her dentures overboard. Thereafter, she refused to appear without them and had puréed food sent to her room.

Dietrich, was soon homesick, she sent and received radiograms from the moment she boarded the S S *Bremen* until disembarking in New York City. Sieber was keeping her up to date, sending one favourable review after another; she was 'the event' of Berlin.[76] All the critics agreed that whilst Jannings was good, he was nothing in comparison to this unrivalled new star. Hardly seeming to care, Dietrich sent him back a stream of longing messages, full of home-sickness and regrets. She took some relief in sending tart messages to von Sternberg in Hollywood. He had been eagerly anticipating her arrival for two months and was expecting rather more gratitude from his muse and protégée.

On board ship, Dietrich was befriended by a young and glamorous American couple, Jimmy and Bianca Brooks, the founders of Jimmy Brook's Costume Company. They spent much time together playing cards and sharing their meals. At first glance Bianca worried that the beautiful German star had designs on her husband, but Dietrich certainly had more than enough adoring men for the moment. Instead she attempted to seduce the bewildered Bianca, sending her the symbolic violets and lesbian literature. Supposedly she told her, *In Europe it doesn't matter if you're a man or a woman. We make love with anybody we find attractive.* 77 This was typical of what Dietrich would have said and indeed of the way she lived her life; America was about to be shocked. Neither her new country nor Bianca Brooks, was quite ready for Dietrich's enthusiasms. Paramount quickly realized they needed to come up with a way of carefully packaging their independent and articulate new star.

Dietrich arrived in New York on 9 April 1930, two days late; a storm had delayed the ship. She was greeted on board by the Paramount Pictures East Coast executives, who would introduce her to America.

Herbert Hoover was president of the United States, and the country was in the depths of the Great Depression. Americans worshipped their film stars especially during this time, as they provided them with an escape from the hardships of their daily lives. Before Dietrich boarded the train for the West Coast, Paramount Pictures had organised a four-day publicity schedule for New York, starting the moment she arrived. Slightly bemused, Dietrich agreed to meet the press, not in her beige suit as she had planned but, on by Paramount's advice, in a black dress and her white mink coat – certainly wrong for ten o'clock in the morning. Sitting her on top of her luggage, the

Marlene Dietrich on her first Atlantic crossing. Her masculine attire, hardly unusual in 1920s Berlin, caused a sensation and an unexpected fashion trend as women flocked to buy trousers

AMERICAN FAME

Unsound business practices and panic selling of shares caused the stock market to crash in October 1929. The situation was worsened by crippling droughts. Not until President Franklin D Roosevelt introduced the 'New Deal' in 1932 did the economic tide turn. One industry that flourished at this time was the film industry; for 10 cents people could escape their daily drudgery for a glimpse of movie magic.

photographers demanded she show off her legs, as if she was simply some plaything for their amusement. She found the whole thing absurd; everyone seemed rude and their questions were impertinent and stupid. She told the journalists that she missed her daughter. This certainly confused them, as stars did not have children. She could not say if she liked America, as she had not yet disembarked. All she really wanted was to find new teeth for her maid Resi, and get the poor girl on shore and off her diet of puréed food.

As soon as they got to their hotel, Resi was whisked off to the dentist. Dietrich sat down to write to Rudi. She was desperately longing for some company other than a toothless maid and the never-ending stream of journalists. Walter Wanger, Paramount's East Coast Head of Production had been instructed to take her out for dinner with his wife. He turned up alone, his wife 'indisposed', and took her to a speakeasy. Dietrich had told journalists in that afternoon's press conference that she adored Harry Richman; Wanger had brought her here so she might hear Richman sing 'On the Sunny Side of the Street'. She was thrilled to hear the singer in real life, whose songs she had played time and time again on her gramophone. However, by the time Wanger tried to fondle her on the dance floor, she had had enough. Excusing herself, she walked out and took a taxi back to her hotel and rang von Sternberg in Hollywood in a rage.[78] He ordered her to get a train out of New York immediately. Dietrich might make love to whomever she found attractive, but she was not to be taken for granted, especially not by one of the producers of the company she was contracted to.

Von Sternberg joined her train in Albuquerque, New Mexico,

and travelled the last stretch with her and Resi. Arriving in Pasadena on 12 April 1930, they left the train in order to avoid any more journalists. Here they were greeted only by the studio-controlled press. This time they would have control of all the photographs, the interviews, and the questions. Von Sternberg had already pre-

Prohibition 1919–33
The 18th Amendment to the constitution made it illegal to manufacture, sell, or transport alcohol in the US. Many otherwise law-abiding citizens completely ignored the ban and drank alcohol, provided by 'bootleggers', in underground clubs called 'speakeasys'. In 1933, the Democratic Party ended 'The Great Experiment'.

pared the press, creating a myth around Dietrich's past that would follow her to her death and still leads to confusion over certain dates and stories in her life even today. The 28-year-old German was, according to von Sternberg, 25 or younger, born somewhere around Berlin. She had a baby, four years old, or sometimes two. Her husband was a film producer, or a director, or an executive. Her father had been German nobility and a Prussian war hero, which practically made her aristocratic. Her name was Maria (or Marie Magdalene) von Losch; 'Marlene Dietrich' was a stage name acquired in order not to offend her upper-class family. She had been a concert violinist but was forced to retire because of an injury to her wrist. Josef von Sternberg had discovered her as a student acting in some small piece by Max Reinhardt . . .[79]

Marlene Dietrich had arrived in Hollywood. She was installed in a small house in Beverly Hills, close to Sternberg's own, which he was still sharing with his wife. The studio provided her with a green Rolls-Royce, two maids, and opened a bank account with $10,000 for her personal use, not that she needed money other than to send home to Berlin. On a diet since she started filming for *The Blue Angel*, Dietrich was eating virtually nothing and, to become even slimmer, was giving herself saltwater emetics. Dietrich had always loved her food and usually gorged herself at meals. The diet she knew was starvation.

To pass the time, she and Resi went to the cinema, she worked in her garden, cooked, and read. At this time, she first encountered *All Quiet on the Western Front*, as a film, rather than the novel. Curious to read her old Viennese friend, Erich Maria Remarque's work, she wrote home to ask Sieber to send her the German edition.

In what seems a selfish need to keep Dietrich devoted to him, von Sternberg convinced her that it was inadvisable to socialize before her command of English was consonant 'with the charm of her looks . . . '[80] Plainly, she would need to be kept out of sight until this obstacle was overcome. The enforced isolation only perpetuated her longing for Maria, her husband, and life in Berlin. Dietrich rang home daily and wrote letters, giving her a desperately needed opportunity of keeping in touch with Germany and the gossip back home. She told Rudi everything, as had always been her habit, even forwarding von Sternberg's letters when they proved informative or interesting. Lonely and bored, she called von Sternberg 'on script revisions' at all hours of the day and night. Royce's tolerance had reached its limit; von Sternberg threw her out.[81] What Dietrich really needed was a film.

Von Sternberg already had a script based on the novel, *Amy Jolly, Woman of Marrakesh*, Dietrich had slipped it into his luggage when he left Berlin. She had met the author, Benno Vigny, while holidaying on the island of Sylt on the North Friesland coast the previous summer with Maria. Dietrich had her doubts. Although the book was an easy read, she felt it was a rather weak story. Such minor details bored von Sternberg as his films were never narrative-driven; this was to be yet another triumph. He called it *Morocco*.

In advance of shooting the film, Paramount Pictures launched a $500,000 publicity campaign to push Dietrich's profile even higher, setting up a blizzard of advertisements, interviews, and portraits. Von Sternberg was even persuaded to shoot one of their promotional trailers, *Paramount on Parade,* in both English and German. Dietrich was famous in the USA long before the American public ever saw her in a film.

In *Paramount on Parade*, she was filmed in shorts, revealing dresses, and white tie and tails. The studio was shocked. Women in America did not wear trousers. Von Sternberg told them not to worry, and, for heaven's sake, not to interfere. He would control Miss Dietrich's image; the trailer, however, seems never to have been released. Blake McVeigh, the publicity man, was instead assigned to get a decent picture for the studio. She told him *I'm loafing around in slacks. If you want to shoot me this way, all right.*[82] He agreed, knowing that the publicity department and just about everyone else were going to object. Then, when he came across a small selection of women's gardening trousers in his local department store, he thought perhaps women other than Dietrich wore or wanted to wear trousers. To the surprise of the studio executives, the photos were in great demand by the press, and within days stores were being besieged by women wanting to try the new look. The star was a fashion sensation. Dietrich found the whole thing amusing; trousers had never been a statement for her, but simply a matter of comfort. Paramount was delighted. They had always worried that Dietrich was going to be thought of as simply another imitation of Greta Garbo but now she had her own look. Dietrich in trousers was no longer a shocking embarrassment but a new publicity campaign: 'The Woman Even Women Can Adore'. The slogan on the posters described her as, 'The Woman All Women Want To See'.[83] Paramount would see to it that Dietrich would be a phenomenon, worth every cent spent on her promotion.

Dietrich met with Head of Costumes at Paramount, Travis Banton, and took charge of her part of the film, and the clothes. Banton matched Dietrich's intensity and her indefatigable determination to find the right look. They worked for hours, often all day and into the night; this was to be the beginning of a long collaboration that lasted until she left Paramount in 1937.

Visually, *Morocco* (1930) is told in a very different style from *The Blue Angel*, even if Dietrich plays yet another showgirl. This stylish film gave her an opportunity to show off a more elegant side. Unlike Lola Lola, Amy Jolly does not wear worn and threadbare clothes, but beautiful dresses. Now Dietrich was a true star, she had a whole department and Banton's dedication to create anything she wanted. But the very first time the whole world was invited to fall in love with her screen image, she wears her own white tie and tails, which von Sternberg had admired at a Berlin party, hiding her by now famous legs. Throughout the rest of *Morocco*, she sports various flowing dresses.

Half-starved, she became more obsessive about her weight; and complained of feeling fatter on less food than ever before. Von Sternberg told her not to worry, but she insisted on wearing slimming black (the most difficult colour to film), trailing a boa whenever possible, behind which she could hide. America had thought the athletic Garbo too fat, but this was not going to happen to Dietrich – she was living off cigarettes, coffee, and vigorous exercise. She was thinner than she had ever been in her life.

Remodelled as 'Marlene Dietrich' by her mentor, Josef von Sternberg, Dietrich was launched by Paramount Pictures launched Dietrich with a huge publicity campaign. She was famous in the USA before they had ever seen her on screen

With the costumes designed, there was very little else for Dietrich to do but wait. Von Sternberg had not given her a script to learn; he told her not to worry, as he would feed her each scene, line by line, thereby controlling her acting completely. To improve her English quickly, he refused to converse with her in German and drilled her daily in English, often reducing her to tears.

They spent most of their time together, continuing their affair, and she relied on him completely for guidance and an introduction into America. Frequently she told him how much she admired him and how she would be nothing without him, but he came to realize that her admiration did not equal love. She would never love him as he loved her. As his obsession grew, he began to punish her for her lack of feeling. Grateful for his expertise and friendship, Dietrich accepted the abuse.

Morocco began filming on 15 July and finished on 18 August 1930. Dietrich starred opposite Gary Cooper (who was given top billing), but by Hollywood's standards, the real star of the film was Adolphe Menjou, as he was paid the highest fee, at $20,000. Gary Cooper was on a similar rate to Dietrich. The total production costs came to an estimated $450,000. The film was shot on a Paramount soundstage, packed with horses, camels and mules, and teeming with extras, filling the faux Moroccan houses and bazaars.

The plot of *Morocco* is extremely thin. Tom Brown (Gary Cooper) is a soldier in the French Foreign Legion. Adored by many, he is remains uninterested in anyone until the arrival of Amy Jolly (Marlene Dietrich). When a millionaire, Kennington (Adolphe Menjou), offers her marriage and respectability, she rejects him and follows Tom Brown, and the Legion, to the front line. Kennington drives her into the desert, where war and certain death await. She walks barefoot, into the sand dunes, in a shot that made movie history. The wind tugs at her dress, as she joins the other soldiers' women, without shoes, hat or food. Tom Brown is unaware of her pursuit. She will die and we all know it; it is classic 1930s Hollywood melodrama. 'Those women must be mad', Amy Jolly says earlier in the film, of the women who followed the soldiers. 'Oh, I don't know,' Kennington answers her. 'You see, they love their men.' By the end, Amy Jolly knows what she wants; even if it means sacrificing herself. Dietrich's performance reveals the complexity of the female condition, as she is in turn independent and vulnerable, a theme that runs consistently throughout the film. From the very first time Amy Jolly sees Tom Brown, she takes control of their affair – her strength fascinates him. In her tailcoat, watched by an intrigued Brown, Amy Jolly borrows a flower from a girl and kisses her on the lips, while the girl giggles delightedly. She then throws the flower to Brown and walks out. The scene is unprecedented in film; never before or since has there been a flirtation, controlled by a woman, as cool and calculated as this. Of course, it is popular today to see this as evidence of Dietrich's bisexuality, although the scene goes beyond sexual orientation. But does this in any way reflect Dietrich's love affairs with women? She uses the flower-girl to empower herself, to play the man's role, enabling her to keep control without offending him. It is neither a lesbian moment nor a feminist one, rather a portrayal of female instinct. Dietrich shows how women use their intuition in their relationships with men. Unlike the men in the film, Dietrich's character knows all the tricks. It was the much the same in life, she was a true survivor. This facet of her nature so obsessed von Sternberg that he felt compelled to capture it on film.

Almost as if von Sternberg had anticipated the inevitable outcome of his relationship with Dietrich, he wrote Menjou's role as if he could have played it himself. Most of the men Dietrich left in his movies, resembled von Sternberg in appearance, social position, or behaviour. They were willing to give her everything – love, devotion, wealth and even respectability – but still she left them. Von Sternberg was extraordinarily perceptive: he recognized that he could provide only a fragment of what she needed. For Dietrich, as for the characters in her films, choosing respectability would have meant destroying the very woman she was.

As if to counterbalance Dietrich's lack of devotion, von Sternberg bound her to him professionally. He ensured that she could not exist without him, placing himself in a position to dominate, humiliate, or protect her at will.

Shooting the first scene of *Morocco* initiated one of the more unsympathetic patterns of the von Sternberg/Dietrich relationship. Dietrich had not seen the script, and was speaking her lines for the very first time on the set. The lighting and costumes were exquisite, and her appearance beautiful. But when she delivered her lines, a strong accent detracted from her sublime image. She could not pronounce 'help' in the line, 'I won't be needing any help' – the first thing her character says to Menjou. Von Sternberg could have dubbed over the problem, blocked out the sound with an effect, used a thousand tricks to cover it up, but instead he insisted that she say it properly. To truly succeed, Dietrich needed to seduce with her voice as well as her looks. His method, however, was unnecessarily brutal. He drove her through 48 takes, shocking the crew and cast with his cruelty, and eroding her confidence. All of this could have been avoided with just one rehearsal prior to shooting. He finally corrected her pronunciation with just a few words: 'Say it like you would in German', he told her, 'pronounce every letter'. She did and at once the tension evaporated. She scrawled, 'The Villain' over the apology he sent to her dressing room, and forwarded it to Sieber without further comment.[84]

Von Sternberg's controlling grip continued throughout the filming. Rather than relying on her talent, he forced emotions like anger and impatience from her by creating an almost method atmosphere on set, shouting and humiliating her until he achieved the effect he desired from the response of her emotions rather than her acting.

At times he would instruct her as if he were a choreographer. His inventive technique was to use numbers; Dietrich wrote home to Sieber recounting his method step-by-step. Von Sternberg would dictate: 'Miss Dietrich, do exactly as I say: Look at him, count one-two, say "You better go now . . ." Move to the door, count one-two-three-four, slowly! Turn, don't look at him, say: "I'm . . ." stop. Count one-two-three-four. Keep your eyes on his face. Don't blink. Then say – slowly – "beginning to like you."' Dietrich added *if . . . you know I am counting one, two, three – it can be very funny*.[85]

She had to admit that although indeed 'villainous', von Sternberg's methods were highly effective, using this counting system, he created some of the most erotically charged shots the studio had ever seen.

Dietrich might not always understand how von Sternberg reached the final result, but she agreed with the basic principle. In order to turn 'Marlene Dietrich' into the greatest star ever, she was willing to endure absolutely anything. In the end, whatever the cost, that was all that mattered to them both. 'Marlene Dietrich' was made by their applied techniques and her determination.

Supported by the make-up department, she helped the Dietrich face using white eyeliner to open the eyes, and a lighter base below the bridge of her nose, to give the illusion it was straight. Under von Sternberg's exacting directing and lighting she literally glowed, so

In my case the face was created. The main spotlight was placed very low and far away from me. The secret face with the hollow cheeks was achieved as a result of placing the main spotlight close to my face and high above it.[86]

much so that false rumours emerged that she used gold dust in her hair to create the glitter.

Although both Dietrich and von Sternberg always insisted that her look was created by his lighting directions, union laws prevented him being named cinematographer. He took all of her publicity stills and controlled every image of her that left the studio. Still, it is fair to say that in *Morocco* the cinematographer Lee Garmes and von Sternberg developed this image together: so romantic, almost

Garbo-esque. 'Only', as a critic pointed out, 'Miss Dietrich is prettier,' and slightly softer and more aloof than she would later become.[87] By the time of *Shanghai Express*, Garmes and von Sternberg's third film together, Dietrich's shadowy look was perfected, with the beautifully lit high cheekbones and the heavy-lidded eyes.

Morocco was a huge commercial and critical hit, returning a two million dollar profit for Paramount Pictures. Dietrich was nominated for her first and only Academy Award, alongside von Sternberg for direction, Lee Garmes for cinematography, and Hans Dreier for art direction. None of them won, but their importance on the Paramount lot was established and Josef von Sternberg was back in favour.

Not wanting to wait, Paramount Pictures rushed the team straight into their next film. Dietrich and von Sternberg started the preparations on their new project before they had finished *Morocco*. Von Sternberg wanted to call it X-27, but it became *Dishonored*. Everything about the film feels rushed: von Sternberg's story, Dietrich's costumes, the acting, and the shooting.

A Viennese spy falls in love with the Russian agent she is investigating. As Gary Cooper refused to work with von Sternberg again, he cast the rather gruff looking Victor McLaglen. The film includes a scene in which Dietrich's character acts the part of a mentally disturbed country maid. A lightweight film, *Dishonored* had little to offer but it made no difference. *Morocco* and *The Blue Angel* were filling the American cinemas; the public were happy to watch her in anything.

Having fulfilled her contract, she took the boat back to visit Germany for four months. She arrived just in time for Maria's birthday on 13 December. Two weeks later Dietrich turned 29. She was a world-famous star, with three successful films released in a single year, two of which remain classics.

To ensure Dietrich's return, Paramount Pictures rushed to extend her contract before she left for Germany. Her income was tripled, she was now guaranteed $250,000 a year for two pictures, bringing her status and salary up to the level of her only true rival, MGM's Greta Garbo.

Dietrich had no desire to remain alone in Hollywood, but to stay in the ever more unstable Germany would have been mad. Not only was her family relying on her income, but she had grown used to luxury and the glamorous life of Hollywood. She would return to Hollywood, but only if von Sternberg could convince Sieber that this time she could bring the six-year-old Maria along too (Dietrich insisted she was four). Germany was changing, and the National Socialists had become a real threat. Sieber, thanks to the status of his famous wife, was being courted by the Nazis. In 1932, he moved to Paris, where he took a job with Paramount Paris, similar to the one he had held with Paramount Berlin, dubbing films into foreign languages.

Rudolf Sieber came to Hollywood on 19 July 1930 to save his wife's reputation. By then Maria had given herself the nickname 'Heidede'

Dietrich and Maria left for Hollywood on 16 April 1931. Upon arrival in the US, in front of the press, a she disembarked from the ship, Dietrich was served with a $500,000 lawsuit from Riza Royce von Sternberg for 'alienation of affection' from her husband, and another $100,000 for libel; in an earlier interview, Dietrich had been quoted as saying that von

Sternberg no longer loved his wife. Dietrich was furious, and quite prepared to leave this *uptight, crazy* country immediately. She was worried that news of the scandal might reach the Berlin press, and that her mother would find out before she could explain herself. Paramount Pictures was at once delighted with the publicity, but also concerned that tags like 'home wrecker' and 'love pirate' were being attached to their star.[88] Dietrich denied all the charges and Paramount quickly moved to promote her role as a mother to persuade the press of her innocence. She was, after all, a wife and mother, returning from a visit to her husband. Her image was salvaged, and the rumours finally squashed, when Sieber appeared (minus Tami) in Hollywood on 19 July 1931, to vindicate his wife. He was met at the station by Dietrich, Maria, and von Sternberg, obviously proving that an affair could not exist. After all, what sort of husband would face the humiliation of accepting his wife's lover? The Viennese journalist admitted to having misquoted Dietrich, putting an end to the case. Paramount paid off Riza Royce with $100,000 and asked Dietrich to send a letter of apology. The case was closed.

Dietrich and Maria were installed in a Spanish-style mansion in Beverly Hills, complete with Olympic-sized swimming pool for *das kind* (the child). Dietrich only ever rented in Los Angeles; to her, Hollywood, no matter how long she stayed there, was always just a place of transit.

Keeping herself under the illusion that Maria was still an infant, Dietrich resisted sending her to school or indeed teaching her English. After all, everyone spoke German in their house. Von Sternberg, knowing personally how frustrating it could be to live as a non-English speaker in America, took on the task of teaching Maria, for one hour a day. Now free from marital obligations, he was able to spend most of his time with them, except when directing, or studio-related business occupied him.

In the midst of von Sternberg's misery in the divorce courts, Dietrich began her first affair in Hollywood. Maurice Chevalier had just returned to Paramount Pictures after the death of his mother, leaving his estranged wife at home in Paris. Soon the two were inseparable, going out dancing and partying. Dietrich, against von Sternberg's jealous advice, had joined the Hollywood party circuit. Chevalier, who was extremely candid about his long list of lovers, always insisted that they had a platonic relationship, as at that time he had not yet divorced.

According to Maria (though admittedly this was a 7-year-old's recollection), Dietrich explained this somewhat differently to Sieber. *[You] know [Chevalier] had gonorrhoea when he was seventeen, that's why he's impotent.* Sieber just laughed, 'Oh, Mutti! They can't ALL have had gonorrhoea.'[89] (Miraculously many of Dietrich's 'medically afflicted' lovers recovered from their illness when she revealed that she preferred kissing, cuddling and romance, and did not mind impotence whatsoever.)[90]

Dietrich and Chevalier enjoyed being together, both longing for European company; they spoke French, discussing European books, culture, and art. Sieber and Chevalier were soon good friends and would meet up in Paris. Von Sternberg fumed with jealousy, going as far as sneaking into the studio at night to destroy the negatives of the many photographs Paramount Pictures were sending out of their two stars. The affair became embarrassing. Chevalier broke it off when his wife initiated divorce proceedings; he did not think it wise for Dietrich to appear in yet another divorce court accused of stealing another woman's husband. Perhaps an affair with Dietrich was just too complicated.

Her return visit to Berlin and Sieber's arrival in Hollywood with Maria had revitalized Dietrich; she felt back in control of her life. Von Sternberg was now displaced. He was no competition for Sieber, and he knew it. Now he had all the time in the world to spend with her, Dietrich no longer wanted to be with him twenty-four hours a day. She needed him as her most skilled director but thought only of their next project.

Shanghai Express (1931), shot in late September, was yet another hit, nominated for three Academy Awards. This time Lee Garmes won an Oscar for cinematography. Regardless of whether the lighting and camera movements were a collaboration between von Sternberg and Garmes or not, the cinematography is inspired, even visionary. The camera seems to float, and the shots meld into, and onto each other in a breathtaking example of visual storytelling. (Alfred Hitchcock was inspired by von Sternberg, and would later adapt this style beautifully.)

Set in China, the story is somewhat banal and its dialogue rather stale. Dietrich plays Madeline, China's most notorious white prostitute, nicknamed Shanghai Lily. She meets up with an old lover on a steam train (a real one, brought into the studio). Dietrich did not care much for her leading man, Clive Brook, but enjoyed working with her female co-star, the Chinese-American Anna May Wong (Wong Liu Tsong). This is the only time that one of Dietrich's film characters has a female friend on screen. Perhaps

Dietrich and Von Sternberg on the set of *Shanghai Express*. They had already begun their venomous fighting

this partnership was possible because Wong was Asian, and although very beautiful, would not upstage Dietrich in the eyes of a white audience. She did not, and their on-screen relationship brings life to the otherwise moribund male performances. The film received glowing reviews, and suddenly everyone was quoting Shanghai Lily's lines all over America. A particular favourite was: 'It took more than one man to give me the name of Shanghai Lily.' This was pure 1930s camp. The audience loved it. Dietrich wears some of her most stunning outfits featuring feathers and veils. Her acting throughout most of the film consists of striking a pose and rolling her eyes.

Dietrich was paid for writing the next von Sternberg/Dietrich film, *Blonde Venus* (1932), but was not given a screen credit. Von Sternberg claims to have conceived the plot 'to provide something other than the sob stories that were being submitted [by the

'Suddenly [von Sternberg] grabbed a comb and parted my hair on the wrong side, bringing the face alive. It's been there ever since.'
CARY GRANT, *Blonde Venus*, 1932

studio].'[91] A story of motherly love and sacrifice, it was Dietrich's first chance to project her idea of what it meant to be a German woman onto the wide screen; independent but always devoted to her husband and child, acting in their best interests out of love and respect.

Most of Dietrich's story survived the censors, aside from a revised ending. Helen Faraday (Dietrich), a cabaret singer is befriended in Germany by an American soldier/scientist, played by Herbert Marshall. When he falls seriously ill, Helen finds the money to send

The Hays Code of self-censorship was adopted by the Hollywood film industry in self-defence against threatened government action. In 1933, the public outcry over violent and sexually suggestive films increased and the 'New Motion Picture Production Code' was introduced. If a film violated the code it would not be distributed. The code limited the sexual content, forbade any religious controversy, and if evil was depicted it was punished, thus encouraging predictable happy endings. Criminals and prostitutes were no longer portrayed as heroes. In the 1960s, the code was replaced by the current rating system.

him to Germany for a cure, by seducing a rich and influential politician, Nick Townsend (Cary Grant – then a young protégé of Mae West. Later, in Hitchcock's *North by Northwest*, Grant would be suspected of killing a character named Townsend). Returning home early, Helen's husband discovers her infidelity and demands a divorce and the surrender of their child. Helen runs from him and the law, singing and seducing her way across America to support herself and her child. Townsend finds her in Paris, now a famous singer, and brings her home, where she lives in harmony with husband, lover, and child.

Paramount approved everything but the ending; as they would never have been able to get it approved by the Hays Office. Offended at having his artistic freedom reduced, von Sternberg resigned from the project and when it was assigned to another director, Dietrich walked off the set. They were both suspended for breach of contract; Dietrich was struck off the payroll and Paramount sued von Sternberg for $100,000. Typically, von Sternberg was only offended that they had not demanded more, and considered counter-suing. Dietrich, never one to worry about money, took the opportunity to relax for a while, taking care of Maria and eating – now that she was under no pressure to stay thin. There was a short period of normal life for the two of them, going to the cinema and the beach.

There can be no doubt that Dietrich was completely devoted to Maria: she expressed this affection by insisting that her daughter accompany her everywhere, and when the studio suggested that she appear without her – as her audience did not want to see an enigmatic star as a mother – simply pulled Maria closer. *This is MY child. She BELONGS to me . . . They don't want her? Then they don't get me!* [93] If Dietrich had been able to raise her daughter under normal circumstances, if Maria had been allowed her own existence and independence, then perhaps the dangerous amalgam of love and insecurity might have had a less damaging effect on the child. But an event was about to happen, that would make it impossible for Maria ever to have a normal childhood.

The kidnapping and murder of world-famous aviator Charles Lindberg's infant son in March 1932 was in every newspaper. On 15 May 1932 Dietrich received the first of three ransom notes threatening Maria's safety and demanding '$10,000 on Lindberg business'.[94] The threat had an electrifying effect on Dietrich who demanded protection from every security agency. Maria was never let out of her sight again. Von Sternberg and Chevalier were expected to guard the house – now barred and gated – fully armed and ready to shoot on sight. Sieber was ordered to come over from Paris, immediately, even though, with all the connections, the journey would take him at least ten days. The whole ordeal was over within two weeks. The copycat kidnappers were amateurs, even managing to confuse the final ransom note they sent Dietrich, with that intended for the parents of another child.

As the ransom was never collected, the FBI closed their files on the case as 'unsolved'. Dietrich hired two full-time bodyguards for Maria and cancelled all plans of ever sending her to school in

California. She was tutored at home and spent most days at the studio with her mother, either on film sets or at dress fittings.

This might have been enough of an education in itself, had she not been reduced to Dietrich's silent companion, knowing no children of her own age and always feeling that she came second and her mother's career first. Dietrich soon came to rely heavily on her daughter and included her permanently in her entourage. Maria's childhood was abruptly over. Mother and daughter shared an uncanny eye for the right look in clothes, and a knack for spotting imperfection. From the age of eight onwards, Maria took on the role of special assistant to Dietrich.

In order for life to return to normal, and to ensure that Dietrich stayed in the US, Dietrich and von Sternberg accepted all of Paramount's restrictions on their new script and went back to work. Sieber returned to Tami and his own life in Paris.

As a gesture of appeasement Paramount Pictures refurbished Dietrich's 1800-square-foot dressing room (including hallway, living room, dressing room, bathroom and make-up room) at a cost of $300,000. (The furniture later ended up in a storage room for years, and is now stored at the Marlene Dietrich Collection in Berlin.)

The ending of *Blonde Venus* was changed; Helen returns to her husband and gives up Nick Townsend so that she might stay with her child. With the von Sternberg/Dietrich creativity curtailed, *Blonde Venus* became a hobbled work. The storyline is in constant conflict with the Paramount-imposed morality and Dietrich is clearly uncertain of her character's motives. She swings from moments of brilliance and control to merely walking through her part. The costumes are mostly a repeat of what Dietrich and Banton had done before and von Sternberg's soft-focus, richly contrasting cinematography, with its over-composed and controlled beauty, overshadows the story's need of realism. Nonetheless, the film remains an interesting study of a woman managing the traditionally male position of working parent – naturally the issue foremost in Dietrich's personal life. The very real conflict is unfortunately trivialized by Helen being forced to return home, leaving behind all of her own needs for those of her child and husband. An exceptional scene, in which Dietrich excels, occurs when Helen, robbed of her child, forced into prostitution, finds herself in a homeless shelter. (This was based on a Bowery doss-house where von Sternberg had stayed when he was 17, with no money.) Not prepared to compromise, Helen throws away her husband's hard-earned money with which he has just repaid his debt to her and her rich lover, implying that her work and the money she earned was never as real as his. Mocking his words and mirroring his impact on her life, she says, as she gives it all to a random stranger: 'In this envelope is $1,500 – it represents my life's work. Had I had time to exploit it properly, I could have made a fortune.' The next time that we see her, she is in vestal-white top hat and tails, flirting with a chorus girl. If Helen succeeded once, she can do it again and this time she is singing to women, free of men. *Blonde Venus*, or whatever is left of it, is truly a woman's film. Its issues are perhaps more topical for today's female viewers than they were for women in the 1930s. Over-directed, over-budget and late, the film suffered on every level. It received a luke-warm reception critically and was commercially disappointing.

Von Sternberg and Dietrich were now fighting openly on set, and Paramount was beginning to question the sense of keeping them together. The Depression affected the studio badly; what they needed was a huge hit from their expensive star. Von Sternberg went to the West Indies to film hurricanes for a circus film, in which he intended to cast Dietrich as a lion-tamer. But he returned to the studio and announced he was retiring from the film business, aged 38, to paint. While he had been away, Dietrich had started affairs with Garbo's lover, the screenwriter Mercedes de Acosta, and her tennis instructor, the great British champion, Fred Perry. Von Sternberg was furious. He knew he had failed her in their last film together, but he could no longer endure their fighting and the emotional turbulence of their partnership; he was exhausted by his jealous obsession with Dietrich. In contravention to his contract with Paramount, he began talks with other studios including UFA in Berlin. He clearly saw the wisdom of a separation from Dietrich though this may, in fact have been a misguided attempt to make her realize how much she depended on him.

Dietrich's natural instinct in judging the quality of the material she was offered was sound, and she had the keenest eye for spotting roles that would increase her lustre; but her extravagance and generosity meant that she could never stop earning. This necessity forced her into many artistic compromises, and in the long term it would come to damage her career. Without von Sternberg's guiding hand she accepted unsuitable contracts, only to realize later that she was trapped. Her attempts at escape were frequently countered by threats of lawsuits from Paramount Pictures and the suspension of her income. An example of this capitulation is her involvement in *Song of Songs* with Rouben Mamoulian in the spring of 1933. The film is a version of Hermann Suderman's already outdated 1908 novel of the same name.

Song of Songs is dreary, it is only really interesting for its underlying theme, which was primarily the result of heavy censoring by the new Production Code. An artist (Brian Aherne, immediately Dietrich's lover) convinces a naïve country girl (Dietrich) to pose for him in the nude and they begin a love affair. His friend, the Colonel (Lionel Atwill), falls in love with her and commissions him to make a statue of the girl. The story is made just that little more repellent by having the girl's scheming aunt (Helen Freeman) effectively sell her off for marriage to the Colonel. After the failure of this marriage, and yet another stint as a prostitute, the model ends up with the artist, the statue lying destroyed on the floor. Throughout the film – ostensibly in the name of art – the camera moves over the sculpted nudes showing the audience, in stone, what they are not allowed to see in flesh, but giving a clear idea of what the artist sees and what he – and later, the Colonel – wants.

This was the first American film in which Dietrich was not seen through the prism of von Sternberg's direction. The critics reacted favourably, but the public were harsher judges and stayed away in droves.

For Dietrich, *Song of Songs* was significant; it represented her first small step towards true independence. She had little faith in Mamoulian, her director, and, if von Sternberg could no longer be there to protect her, she would have to take control herself of how 'Marlene Dietrich' was presented. If von Sternberg had hoped his absence would have made Dietrich realize her need of him, he was wrong. One of her basic principles had always been that, even if the story was bad, she could at least be beautiful and know her place and her role. For the first time, unable to depend on her director to give her exact line readings as von Sternberg had done, she had to memorize her entire role. With her usual determination and a good memory – from her years as a musician, and stage actress – she learned the script quickly, by simply reading over it several times. She only really cared about her own character; making the ensemble work was the director's job.

When after a sixth take she had been given no guidance or proper directions by Mamoulian, Dietrich became desperate. Unable to contain herself, she whispered into the amplified microphone, her voice reaching every corner of the set, *Jo – where are you?*[95] Mamoulian had not even bothered to make her look beautiful, she thought she looked fat. She decided to learn quickly and make her way on her own.

Dietrich spent the following day analyzing *Morocco* and *Shanghai Express*, watching them repeatedly, learning the set-up for every shot, the optimum position of every light. She never took down a note; she considered that was for people *too dumb to remember.*[96] The next morning she arrived early on set. Using a large full-length mirror positioned right next to the camera, she set the lights with the expertise of a trained cinematographer. Mamoulian took it calmly, simply complimenting her, and allowed the crew to applaud her work. In all probability he knew the cost of contradicting

Dietrich. It is highly likely that Mamoulian joined Dietrich's list of lovers, which would explain the ease with which he excused her behaviour and the liberties she took on the set.

From then on, when filming, Dietrich was in charge, and she would never be controlled or patronized again, unless it suited her purposes. Her relationship with von Sternberg – and all her directors – changed forever. Although she still admired him, he was no longer irreplaceable or infallible.

SCREEN GODDESS 1933–1935

With *Song of Songs* completed, Dietrich, Maria, and her entourage left for Europe in May 1933, on an eagerly anticipated holiday. Just before, von Sternberg had been in Berlin negotiating with UFA Studios to bring himself and Dietrich back to Germany. Sieber, now permanently in Paris, thought it not only unwise but increasingly unsafe for Dietrich to return to Berlin, even for a holiday; the National Socialists had begun to ban her films. Paramount Pictures had relocated most of its Berlin employees to Paris, and, no matter what von Sternberg believed, as a Jew he placed himself in danger by staying in Berlin as long as he did.

The family met in Paris. Dietrich was contracted to make a recording for Polydor of six German and French songs; a contract that Sieber had organized, as once again her need for money was pressing. Many of the German Jewish musical and cinematic talents were leaving Germany: the actor Peter Lorre; her old friends from *The Blue Angel*, Franz Wachsman and Friedrich Hollaender; Mischa Spoliansky; Jan Lustig; and the soon to be famous lyricist Max Kolpe (later Colpet).

Staying at Hôtel Trianon Palace in Versailles, she recorded the new songs composed by Wachsman and written by Kolpe for Polydor. In Paris, she stocked up on clothes, going to fitting after fitting. She met up with Brian Aherne, but her simple devotion to Sieber confused him so much that at first he found it difficult to continue their affair and returned to London. He, too, was unaccustomed to sharing a lover.

The Sieber family went on to Salzburg to meet with Josefine, Liesel, and her son. Dietrich had been trying to persuade her mother to leave Germany for years, but Josefine consistently refused. Like many Germans, when presented with the opportunity to leave, she refused to turn her back on her home, her family, her friends, and her livelihood. Whilst the Nazis were clearly dangerous, she felt sure that their time in office would be short. She returned to Germany, and the Siebers went on to Vienna, a city that Dietrich adored. There, she started an affair with the 28-year-old Viennese actor, Hans Jaray. This was the final straw for Brian Aherne, he joined the ranks of the many lovers with whom she stayed in touch.

Whenever Dietrich wanted to placate or seduce someone, or take control of a relationship, she would cook. The real-life roles of *Hausfrau* and mother were among Dietrich's favourites. She would often feed her lovers and friends, pampering them with their favourite dishes, and bringing them her special beef tea. The domestic goddess combined with her extraordinary beauty, made her irresistible to many. Ever since the first days of filming *The Blue Angel,* she had given von Sternberg lunch in her dressing room. Lovers spent the night and were ushered out before dawn, so as not to upset 'the child', they would then return for breakfast and Dietrich's scrambled eggs, which were famous in Hollywood. Playing the *Hausfrau* role, Dietrich enjoyed cooking and cleaning and helping others. As this was in contrast to her alluring on-screen image, it inevitably surprised the recipients of such attention.

Dietrich was back in Hollywood by mid-September, with a newly-signed contract with Paramount Pictures. Von Sternberg was once more contracted as her director. He had seen her disastrous appearance in *Song of Songs* and he hoped she might need him once more; he had apologised for the months of tantrums and fighting and was preparing for their next film, *The Scarlet Empress,* based on the life of Catherine the Great.

Whilst von Sternberg agonized over the script and created a bizarre gothic set for the Tsarina's palace, with colossal sculptures and doors ten feet tall, Dietrich and Banton conceived some of the most spectacular costumes she would ever wear – furs, enormous hats and hooped skirts. The dresses are masterpieces of the grotesque.

Dietrich's daughter, Maria, was cast the young Sophia Frederica, a poor German princess who would become Catherine the Great, Empress of Russia. Maria was filmed in lying in bed so as to appear younger than her nine years. Her face frozen into a rictus of pain and anger, she delivers her few lines quite acceptably. As Maria was now a Paramount Pictures child actor, she was protected by the studio's strict labour laws. Much to Dietrich's indignation, she now had to accept that Maria was given regular English tuition. Maria was still taught at home but her lessons were subject to the vagaries of Dietrich's need for her daughter's assistance and, consequently her tuition was erratic. Considering the benefits Dietrich had derived from her own very structured education, it was ironic that she could neglect her daughter's. Perhaps, this kept alive the illusion that Maria was still a young child, thereby extending Dietrich's youth.

Meanwhile von Sternberg, frustrated by his longing for Dietrich, started an affair with his secretary. Dietrich was distressed. He had lied about his absolute devotion to her, now he dared to love someone else. The game began again: she now had the freedom to do what she liked, without giving any regard to von Sternberg and, at the same time, could hate him for his infidelity. They fought through letters, and at home, but his most viscious revenge took place on the set. He had Dietrich ring in Catherine's victory 50 times; the bell rope lacerated her legs. That night, limping with pain, she cooked him his favourite Hungarian goulash with broad egg noodles, whilst telling him not to worry. She never tired of their masochistic emotional games and he was quite unable to keep himself from playing them, too.

Despite, Dietrich and von Sternberg's fighting, *The Scarlet Empress* is a magnificent piece of work. Even the historically inaccurate plot works within the exaggerations of the film. Catherine, disappointed in her marriage to the half-witted Tsar, seduces the most important generals and princes, ensuring their loyalty, when she usurps the throne after her husband's death.

The film failed spectacularly. In 1934, audiences were not looking for imperial Russian excesses. The Great Depression at its height, F D Roosevelt had been elected to change the country's fortunes and cinema audiences cried out for homely escapism; Paramount had misfired. In years to come, the extravagance and sweep of the film would be admired and treasured. At the time that did not help Dietrich and von Sternberg.

Paramount Pictures deflected most of the criticism that the film received and directed it at von Sternberg, insisting that Dietrich merely acted as she was told. Von Sternberg was an easy figure to hate, as he was self-consciously convinced of his own brilliance, arrogant, and prone to self-pity. People regularly walked off his sets and despised his self-proclaimed genius and perfectionism; although the results were often brilliant, his means of achieving them crossed the boundaries of abuse of his crew and cast.

Dietrich went back to Paris and comforted herself with an array of lovers and bought herself a set of green emeralds. She met Ernest Hemingway on the boat coming back. He named her 'the Kraut', she called him 'Papa' and although one of her dearest friends, he never became her lover. They remained in close touch until, in 1961, he shot himself.

That summer, Sieber's mistress Tami decided that she was no longer prepared to be hidden within the household. Her official role was that of governess to Maria, so naturally she could have no life of her own, and certainly she could never get pregnant, so suffered regular abortions. In addition she was the butt of Sieber's feelings of inadequacy and frustration. As she loved him, Maria, and possibly Dietrich too, she endured this demeaning situation for many years;

eventually she suffered a mental breakdown. She died in a California state mental institution, in March 1965, allegedly murdered by another patient. Sieber buried her in the Russian Orthodox section of Hollywood Memorial Park Cemetery. He had the inscription 'My Beloved' placed on to her gravestone.[97]

The Devil Is a Woman (1934), Lubitsch's title for *Capriccio Espagnol,* was the last film Dietrich made with von Sternberg. 'She and I have progressed as far as possible together,' he explained, 'and my being with her will help neither her nor me.'[98]

They had been equal in creating the Dietrich legend, but many in the film industry doubted her ability to succeed without him. Sieber had come to Hollywood with Tami to work as an (uncredited) assistant to von Sternberg, but even he could not keep the pair from fighting so severely that they destroyed their relationship on the set. The story of the film is of little consequence, aside from what it tells us of von Sternberg's state of mind.

The film is set in Spain, and told mostly in flashback. Don Pasqual (Lionel Atwill, von Sternberg's double) warns the young Cesar Romero (Antonio Galvan) not to fall for Concha Perez (Dietrich) as she causes nothing but despair and disaster.

Dietrich thought she would never again be as beautiful as she was in this film, it was the only time she would buy a print of one of her films. Von Sternberg finally took credit for both photography and directing. The cinematography throughout the film is beautiful, Dietrich is ravishing, complemented by Banton's spectacular and elegant costumes and make-up. It is a feast for the eyes. For the first time since *The Blue Angel,* von Sternberg portrays Dietrich's character with fatalistic clarity; his depression can be felt in every shot. The fact that Concha Perez never acknowledges the pain she causes the world, gives the film a powerfully obsessive atmosphere, as it traps the lovers (and the audience) in the web of Dietrich's beauty.

The film was panned by critics and audiences alike, who could not warm to Dietrich playing a woman without integrity. A bad situation was considerably worsened when the Spanish government complained about the film, and banned it in Spain, claiming that it was a travesty of Spanish life. The US State Department was so worried that the delicate Spanish–American relationship might be harmed, that they forced Paramount Pictures to destroy, or at least to withdraw the negatives.

Ernest Lubitsch, Head of Production at Paramount, had never liked von Sternberg. When von Sternberg announced his intention to leave both Dietrich and the studio, Lubitsch was quick to let him go. Dietrich had waited to renew her contract in case von Sternberg wanted them to sign with another studio. He decided, however, that he could not risk working with her again. He withdrew to his house in the country; without her, his biggest inspiration, his muse, he was unable to restart his career. In 1943, he married his 21-year-old secretary and they had two children. Even with the passing of a decade, Dietrich was still annoyed. Publicly she always spoke of him with awe and respect; he did not return the compliment, resenting what he suspected was her cynicism. Von Sternberg was stung by the failure of their last collaboration and the exhausting complications of their emotional lives. He found it hard to accept that although she had always respected his talents as a director, she had been indifferent and possibly despised everything else about him.

The now Nazi-controlled German press was quick to use the split from von Sternberg to prove that Dietrich finally shared their views on Jews. They promised her, for all the world to see, that her fatherland was waiting to take her back, to make her into a glamorous representative of the Third Reich, rather than ending her career in the US, 'the tool of Hollywood's Jews!'[101] Up until now, she had refused to take a public stand either for or against Germany in the press. She was now forced to make a statement, perhaps less for personal reasons than to

I was born a German, and I shall always remain German . . . I had to change my citizenship when Hitler came to power. Otherwise I would not have done it. America took me into her bosom when I no longer had a native country worthy of the name, and I am thankful to her for it . . . but in my heart I'm German.[99]

'So few ever understood my mother's ability to view herself in the third person – a Thing, a Superior Product to be continuously scrutinised for the slightest imperfection . . .'
MARIA RIVA[100]

safeguard her future career in America. To clarify her position against Hitler and her opposition to everything Nazi Germany stood for, she made one of the most difficult decisions of her life. After seven years in the US, she decided to renounce her German passport and apply for American citizenship. The anti-Semitic paper, *Der Stürmer* responded: 'The German-born film actress Marlene Dietrich has spent so many years among Hollywood's film Jews that she has now become an American citizen. Here we have a picture in which she is swearing an oath at Los Angeles. What the Jewish "judge" thinks of the formula can be seen from his attitude as he stands in his shirt-sleeves. He is taking the oath from Dietrich, the oath by which she betrayed the fatherland'.[102]

Achilles Heel. Who hasn't got one! The important thing is to be aware of one's Achilles Heel and live with it – not fight it.[103]

Comeback

ABANDONED 1935–1937

As soon as filming was complete and the studio stills from *The Devil Is a Woman* had been taken, von Sternberg took a holiday. Dietrich threw herself into the Hollywood party scene, in an attempt to 'get over the shocking desertion of her creator'.[104] Her professional life seemed to be disintegrating and with von Sternberg's withdrawal, she felt the need more than ever before to be adored. Sieber was leaving for France and, worse still, she could no longer pretend that Maria was a baby. Dietrich could no longer lie about her daughter's age, and Maria, surprising many, aged from five to eleven years of age in a single evening. Dietrich might still be playing young women in her films, but in life she was aging; Maria was the proof of that. The need to be in love had become more than a necessity, it was central to her existence. In 1935, a vintage year for passionate encounters, she entertained many of her regular lovers and added several new ones, including: the Spanish pianist and movie star, José Iturbi; the director and old friend, Fritz Lang (whom she would later come to hate); one of D W Griffith's silent stars, Richard Barthelmess; the distinguished British actor, Ronald Colman; the actor and screen partner of Greta Garbo, John Gilbert; and, possibly just as a friend, the New York socialite, Countess Dorothy di Frasso, American-born daughter of a New Jersey millionaire, Bertrand Taylor.

'How is it possible for a mortal to balance adulation of the most profligate sort with the apparently cruel submission required to retain that admiration?' von Sternberg questioned astutely in his autobiography.[105] Maintaining the illusion was increasingly difficult but for the legend to be sustained it had to appear effortless. When Dietrich felt inadequate, she blamed it on herself and, by extension, von Sternberg, and yet expected him to smooth her path. With time passing and von Sternberg gone, her need for perfection crystallized. She had begun to believe in her own myth, and her many lovers were there to reassure her of the undeniable truth: that Marlene Dietrich was irresistible. Sieber understood, more that any other that the key to loving Dietrich was to accept what she could give, but make no further demands. She was a woman to be adored, not possessed. She always loved with great intensity, but had no patience with jealousy.

Ernst Lubitsch hoped that *Desire* (1935) would save Dietrich's image and bring the public round to loving her again. Originally, he intended to direct the film himself, but because of other production commitments was obliged to hand the direction to Frank Borzage (1893–1962), director of *A Farewell in Arms*. A talented American, Borzage was known for his sentimental approach to romantic dramas. However, Dietrich never thought of him as anything more than a mere assistant to Lubitsch.

With the help of her co-star, Gary Cooper (their first time together on screen since *Morocco*), the film became an opportunity to show off Dietrich's sharp comic timing. Her costumes, for once, take second place to the narrative. She plays Madeleine, a jewel thief who, through a classic movie conceit, steals a valuable pearl necklace from a jeweller in Paris. Mistakenly it ends up in the pocket of Bradley (Cooper), an American tourist on holiday. Madeleine spends the rest of the film getting the necklace back and falling in love with Bradley, while her accomplice, Carlos (John Halliday) arranges for the sale of the pearls. Madeleine regrets her ways, the necklace is returned, and she marries Bradley. The film was originally meant to end at this point, but the Hays Office insisted that Madeleine was a thief who must pay for her crime. To show that she has been rightly punished, Bradley mistakenly hands over her parole papers and not the licence.

Gary Cooper and Marlene Dietrich on the set of *Desire* (1936). Although a posed still, Dietrich loved and excelled in the minutiae of film production

Denied the pleasure of good lighting and elaborate costumes, Dietrich was bored. She did enjoy her reunion with Cooper who, no longer married, was able to 'visit her dressing room'.

If nothing else *Desire* taught her to drive in front of a back projection. Much of the film takes place in cars as characters chase each other over Spanish mountains and through villages. Dietrich had only ever been chauffeured, so could not match the projected scenery behind her. She turned left when the film turned right.

After a morning of failure, Borzage was ready to give up in despair. Not prepared to accept defeat, Dietrich made her favourite grip – at work on a nearby set – teach her how to drive and shift gears during the lunch hour. Sworn to secrecy, he was paid for his troubles. Back on set, she drove her few yards with assurance.

For the first time she lit her own studio stills. Now independent, she was in control of every part of her career previously organized by von Sternberg. The film was well received and both critics and audiences enjoyed seeing a rather more human Dietrich in a light-hearted role. But although she was once again popular at the box office, she could not rival the appeal of Shirley Temple.

Lubitsch rushed her straight into the next production, *Hotel Imperial,* which at the time of shooting was called *Invitation to Happiness,* then becoming *I Loved a Soldier.* Over the course of the film, Dietrich's character metamorphoses as she falls more deeply in love, becoming more beautiful. She liked the concept and the physical demands it made on her appearance, and she liked the young director, Henry Hathaway who had previously worked with von Sternberg.

Halfway through production, Lubitsch was fired by Paramount Pictures, blamed for various studio failures, including the $900,000 that he spent on 28 days of filming only few scenes of *I Loved a Soldier*. Dietrich walked off the set. Her lawyers argued that Paramount was in breach of contract by firing Lubitsch: that he and no other was allowed to supervise her films. They might have been right, but it damaged her career. Dietrich's insistence on complete control was doing no one any good, least of all herself.

Unsure of what to do with Dietrich next, Paramount allowed her to work for an independent producer, David O Selznick for his first Technicolor film, *The Garden of Allah* (1936). He thought he recognized a potential in her that previous directors and producers had missed. As *Desire* had not yet been released, he expected to get her at a lower fee. But by the time contracts were being drawn up her films were doing well enough again at the box office to greatly increase acting fees. Undeterred, Selznick was determined to use her and agreed to pay Paramount a fee of $200,000 for her loan, making her one of the highest-paid stars in Hollywood.

Dietrich took little notice of David O Selznick. At their first meeting, he obviously idolized her but his insistence on drawing attention to what considered were faults in her acting, and the manner in which she had been directed previously, bored her. Dietrich also seriously doubted that the Polish stage director, Richard Boleslawski – hired to direct *The Garden of Allah* – would be her saviour any more than Henry Hathaway had been, despite the fact that she and Boleslawski shared a similar background (he had worked in Berlin in the 1920s).

The Garden of Allah was doomed from the outset. Not even someone of Selznick's talent could save it. An adaptation from Robert Hichens's 1904 novel, which, though shocking when it was published, seemed an anachronism by 1936. The story is set in the Sahara Desert, where Domini Enfilden (Dietrich) has travelled in search of religious solace. She meets a Trappist monk, Boris Androvsky (Charles Boyer) who has fled from his monastery. Boris has realized that he desires more than a life of silent contemplation, he had dreams of love and marriage, even before he met Domini. After they marry, she learns of his past. Tormented by the thought of his broken vows she gives him up. Tearfully, she sends him back to his monastery and he, turning his back on her, happily embraces his silent faith.

The script is inadvertently comic including lines such as: 'Only God and I know what is in my heart.' The cast appear to sleepwalk their way through the film, and Dietrich gives a wholly unconvincing performance as a devout Roman Catholic. She was indifferent to religion in her private life, and she certainly could not portray spiritual devotion on-screen.

The cast and crew worked in the Mojave desert, in Yuma, Arizona where the temperature rose to 103°F in the shade. Consequently, they could shoot only in the morning, as the film would have melted in the cameras in the afternoon heat. Despite a laboratory being on location, it was much too hot to develop the film there. To save the project, Selznick sent long pages of memoranda on each day's filming as it arrived in Hollywood, trying to motivate the actors, and to encourage Boleslawski to take better charge of the shoot. Most of all Dietrich had to stop worrying about the dialogue and her hair. But, as was often the case, Dietrich compensated for a bad script by dazzling with her costumes and carefully planning her poses. There was never an excuse for underachieving, even if everyone around her was doing so. She found Selznick's costume designer mediocre, and secretly she and Travis Banton designed and made nearly all of the costumes on the Paramount lot. She tracked down von Sternberg for his advice; he told her that, until the techniques of filming in colour improved, she needed to think in contrasts, light and dark, just as she would when filming in black and white. The rare treat of seeing Dietrich filmed in colour and the results of her work with Banton are a sensation. Dietrich chose her palette with care. Instead of throwing colour at the audience, simply because it was available, she took a more subtle approach using

The Rise of Facism in Europe

1919: The Italian Fascist Party is founded by Mussolini. Friedrich Ebert becomes first president of the German Republic.

1921: Adolf Hitler becomes leader of the Nazi Party.

1923: Primo de Rivera takes power in Spain.

1928: Mussolini becomes dictator of Italy.

1933: José Antonio Primo de Rivera forms Spanish Falange Part. Hitler is appointed chancellor of Germany. In May, student and members of the Nazi Party burn banned literature on bonfires in Berlin.

1934: Hindenberg dies and Hitler becomes Führer. Night of the Long Knives in which Hitler has many of his opponents killed.

1935: Jews are deprived of German citizenship.

1936: German forces enter demilitarized Rhineland. Germany forms alliances with Italy and Japan. 17 July, Spanish Civil War, Fascism versus Socialism. The Nationalists (supporting fascism) won.

1938: Germany annexes Austria and the Sudetenland. November, Nazi mobs attack Jewish property and synagogues all over Germany.

colours that blended with the landscape. Dietrich had no choice but to wear some of the creations of Ernest Dryden, the credited costume designer, which serve only to throw the success of Banton and Dietrich's collaboration into sharper relief. His designs are awkward and badly cut, and not improved by his uninspired use of colour.

Once again Dietrich's contract ensured that her daughter was on the set at all times, and to alleviate Maria's boredom, it was arranged that she take a minor and role as one of the girls at the convent school.

News from the desert film set went from bad to worse as the international cast struggled with the English dialogue. Desperate to salvage something from this situation, Selznick hired Joshua Logan, a dialogue coach from New York, to improve the cast's delivery. It was to be an uphill struggle as Dietrich's German accent was joined by Boyer's French; C Aubrey Smith was English, and there was a token American, John Caradine; in addition to two Austrians. Logan would later entertain Hollywood with stories of Dietrich's runaway egotism and the notorious desert shoot. Many of the actors succumbed to sunstroke, and suffered with water and food poisoning. Even the director, Boleslawski was taken ill. Dietrich, who never in her career showed any sign of exhaustion from work, finally brought the nightmare to an end by pretending to faint and fall off a horse. Selznick agreed to finish the film back in Hollywood, even it it meant importing several tons of sand from Arizona – California sand was the wrong colour. When *The Garden of Allah* opened in the autumn of 1936, the reviews were kind to both Dietrich's beauty and the new Technicolor. It won an Oscar for its colour cinematography. But the critics had nothing good to say about her acting. One reviewer memorably called her 'a mono-syllabic clothes horse'.[106]

Six days after the completion of the film, on 7 July, Dietrich and Maria were sailing to England on the SS *Normandie*, accompanied this time by Nellie Manley, Dietrich's Paramount hairdresser.

Dietrich had been hired by her old Berlin director, the now London-based Alexander Korda, to star alongside Robert Donat in *Knight Without Armour* (1936), for the unprecedented sum of $450,000. This made her the highest-paid female actress in the world. Despite Korda's reputation and his energies, *Knight Without Armour* was not considered a masterpiece.

Robert Donat plays A J Fotheringill, an British secret agent who, after being released from Siberia at the fall of the Tsarist government, becomes a Bolshevik in order to continue his work. Despite considerable risk to his own life, he saves Countess Alexandra (Dietrich), a White Russian, from execution and they spend much of the film escaping through the countryside. Dietrich is clearly in her element playing a White Russian noblewoman; the chemistry between the leading actors was noted by the critics.

Dietrich takes one of film history's most infamous baths; tales surrounding its shooting, were denied by Dietrich to Maria. Having fled across the country for days, the Countess is offered a bath. To give the illusion of nudity it was usual to wear a flesh-coloured leotard when shooting bathing scenes. According to the newspapers, Dietrich was naked in the bathtub, and on one of the takes, she slipped on her way out of the bathtub and fell. The cameraman, Jack Cardiff, gave this account: 'What does a gentleman do when a world-famous beauty is lying stark naked at his feet, unable to get up? Everyone was much too embarrassed to help her and, still naked, she limped off to her dressing room accompanied by her hairdresser and two hopelessly flustered maids.'[107] According to Maria the story is a fake, nothing but spurious publicity or wishful thinking released to sell the film. Dietrich never showed her naked body to anyone, not even to lovers, and certainly not to film crews. 'Dietrich', she writes, 'young or old, had terrible breasts – they hung, drooped, and sagged.' She was taped or held up by every kind of brassiere and later foundation garments, to give the illusion that her 'ugly breasts' were the 'the pert, upstanding young glands she so desired'.[108] The stories that Dietrich swam naked in her Hollywood pool or stripped to have her beauty appreciated, however much they seem to tally with American ideas of European behaviour and morality, were always denied by her daughter.

Dietrich stayed in Britain for about eight months, her lengthiest stay in Europe since she had left Berlin for Hollywood. When Donat fell ill with asthma for nearly two months in the middle of filming, she insisted that the whole production should be delayed until he recovered. She did not want to relinquish her handsome co-star and lose their on-screen chemistry. This gesture served her well; it was a well-known secret among the British film industry and much appreciated by Donat and his family.

Dietrich enjoyed life in London and was in no particular rush to return to the vicissitudes of Hollywood. Unfortunately for her, Donat was a married man and she had been forced to give up her hope of an affair from their very first cup of tea together. Instead, Korda introduced her to the 26-year-old Douglas Fairbanks Jr. They had met before in Hollywood, but had never been more than casual acquaintances. He too was acting in London and and had divorced one of Dietrich's *bête noires*, Joan Crawford, two years previously. Meeting again, Dietrich was immediately smitten, if not by love, then definitely by lust. Fairbanks Jr was the playboy son of Douglas Fairbanks, who, though an American, was a prominent anglophile.

Fairbanks Jr soon became Dietrich's most famous escort, the press enjoying the affair almost as much as the couple themselves. In the name of respectability, she rented the flat below his penthouse on Grosvenor Square. Hoping that this ruse would avoid embarrassing episodes when he left her hotel in the morning still in evening dress. He was besotted, years later he recollected, 'I couldn't possibly say that I was really in love at the time, but it was certainly a relationship of more sophisticated intensity than any I had so far experienced.'[109] In 1937 however, he was very much in love, sending her *billets doux* and writing reams of love letters daily. Fairbanks appealed to Dietrich's aristocratic pretensions. Through him, she

'[Marlene and I] were to stay at an Austrian chalet on a zee, near a quaint village ... I looked forward to this trip with the world's most desirable woman with great excitement. There was only one drawback. The lovely chalet, rented for a month, was to be shared! And shared, by God, by Marlene's husband, Rudi, and his mistress, Tami. Such a real-life design for living was quite beyond my frame of reference and I protested quietly and grumbled. But it did no good and soon it became evident that Marlene and Rudi were indeed only technically married. They behaved together like old friends and siblings.'
DOUGLAS FAIRBANKS JR.[110]

was introduced to English society. She took a particular interest in the royal family, so much so that the night that Edward VIII announced his abdication, Dietrich tried to meet the young king. To her death, she maintained that had she only been allowed past the guards at the Buckingham Palace gates, she could have changed Edward's mind, no doubt using her own inimitable charms. If only she had been given the opportunity, Edward would have chosen the crown over his emotional needs. For Dietrich, duty and work, were always more important than emotions.

Knight Without Armour opened to hostile reviews, and did not recover its enormous budget. To Dietrich, who had never worried about critics or box office returns, it seemed more important that she had made an enormous amount of money. But after yet another major flop, her career was in trouble. In addition, Korda could not pay her an outstanding $100,000. She agreed to forfeit the amount, providing Korda gave von Sternberg the job of directing *I, Claudius* with Charles Laughton and Merle Oberon, without mentioning her influence. Von Sternberg needed work, as he had only directed two poor films for Columbia since he had last worked with Dietrich. *I, Claudius* was never finished, a combination of von Sternberg's difficult personality, which had worsened as his career declined, and an untimely motor accident involving the star Merle Oberon, brought filming to an end. Korda was able to cancel mid-picture and thus collect the insurance. Von Sternberg's career was over. Tragically, he never managed to recreate the magic he had with Dietrich with any other actress, and always blamed her for his professional decline.

While Dietrich's spent the summer in London conducting her affair with Fairbanks Jr and the filming of *Knight Without Armour*, Maria had been sent to her father, but Sieber did not want to take responsibility for his daughter for more than the holidays. He said that Tami was being impossible and he worried that Maria was now old enough to blame her father for the situation.[111] With the ignorance of the 1930s, Sieber and Dietrich unknowingly encouraged Tami towards a drug addiction with daily amphetamines followed by sleeping pills to sedate her. She was sent to spas for abortions with monotonous regularity and her mental state rapidly deteriorated.

Maria's adolescence was also giving Dietrich cause for concern. Although a quiet and obedient girl, always trying to serve and please her mother, she had reached puberty and was gaining weight and height. Without the discipline of the studio system to fall back on, Dietrich decided to opt for British upper-class solution and find a boarding school. She sent Maria off to Brilliamont, in Switzerland. If Maria could not conform to the 'Dietrich' physical ideal, she could at least learn perfect French. As it turned out this was hardly a punishment. Although Maria had no experience of girls her own age, she, like any teenager, she rejoiced in her new freedom and a life away from her parents.

Dietrich finished her stay in Europe by having affairs with both Colette and Gertrude Stein during the family Christmas holiday in Paris.

In the spring of 1937, Dietrich took Maria out of school early and returned to Hollywood to start shooting *Angel* at Paramount Pictures. She had pursuaded Douglas Fairbanks Jr to take the role of Count Rupert of Hentzau in David O Selznick's *The Prisoner of Zenda*, and to rent a house close to hers. Although he had been reluctant to take a supporting role, she, and his normally disinterested father, Douglas Fairbanks Sr, convinced him that the role would make him more famous. As soon as Fairbanks was back in Hollywood, Dietrich lost interest in him; he had thought there was a chance of replacing Sieber, but no one ever would succeed in that, and he faded from her life.

Ernst Lubitsch directed her in her next movie, *Angel* (1937). Either he had lost the famous 'Lubitsch touch' or perhaps the Hays Code was making subtlety impossible. It was a failure, and one she could ill afford. A formulaic and cliché-ridden plot sees Dietrich's character caught up in a love triangle with Herbert Marshall and Melvyn Douglas. Dietrich lost interest with every facet of the production, even the costumes. Instead, she amused herself with the crew and provided cakes for everyone. Melvyn Douglas remembered, '[the shoot] was like old home week every day.'[112]

In May 1937 a group of independent cinema owners put an advertisement in the *Hollywood Reporter* listing the actors and actresses whom they considered 'box-office poison'. The list included, among others, Joan Crawford, Bette Davis, Marlene Dietrich, Greta Garbo, Katherine Hepburn, and Fred Astaire. This attack was aimed at the studios' control of the industry and in particular the practice of block booking. The cinema owners felt that they were being forced to accept a string of mediocre films – made only as an excuse to parade the studios' expensive stars in uninspired performances – alongside the few profitable films they really wanted. This was damaging to all the actors named, perhaps unfairly, as actors had very little say as to which films and parts they were assigned. Dietrich had the right to veto a script, but she was also under contract to make two films a year.

Infuriated by the 'idiots' of America, Dietrich packed up her Hollywood life, stored her car, and took herself, Maria, Nellie, and Maria's bodyguard back to Europe for a holiday.[113] They spent the summer in Salzburg with Tami and Sieber. They stayed in Austria, where she saw her mother and sister for the last time until the end of the war. Her mother still refused to leave Germany.

After the summer holiday, Maria was sent back to her Swiss school and Dietrich returned to Hollywood in an effort to rebuild her career. According to her contract, Paramount Pictures still owed her a film. Eventually they fired her by paying her $250,000 *not* to act in her next scheduled film, *French Without Tears*. Plans at Columbia Pictures for her to play George Sand were also cancelled. She remained in the USA, needing to spend the requisite period of time in the country to gain her citizenship. Hollywood had become too expensive for her, so she left for Europe as soon as she could. To continue with her application for citizenship, and to travel, she needed to renew her German passport. At the German embassy in Paris, she reassured the envoy sent by the Nazi Party's propaganda minister, Joseph Goebbels, that unfortunately she could not return to Germany, as she still had contracts with American studios, but perhaps she might go back soon; she denied ever wanting an American citizenship, whereupon she, Sieber, and Maria were given passports by the Reich.

The world was watching Germany as refugees fled across Europe, fearing war. Dietrich dallied from city to city. She had a brief fling with American Ambassador to Britain, Joseph Kennedy, while they were holidaying in the south of France, and started an affair with her old friend, the writer, Erich Maria Remarque, whose book had been burned by the Nazis. She might be box office poison but neither fans, nor fame had turned their back on her.

Dietrich at Cap d'Antibes

On 6 June 1939, Dietrich was back in the US to receive her certificate of citizenship, along with 200 other applicants. As a result of her application to become a citizen, she knew that, from January on, the Inland Revenue Service (IRS) would audit her income and was claiming back taxes of $180,000 on her English income. But she affected surprise when Sieber and she were stopped as they boarded the S S *Normandie* bound for France on 14 June. The IRS required her to pay $142,193. Her luggage was taken off, put back, taken off again, all while the worried crew of the S S *Normandie* watched the tide. With the help of her lawyers, it was agreed that if she gave the IRS her jewels, valued at about $108,000 or more, she would avoid arrest and be allowed to leave. Knowing the money was already spent, Dietrich claimed the IRS had miscalculated her tax for all the years she worked in America and, in fact, owed her money. In 1941, she had her jewels returned along with a useful $23,000 rebate.

Liaison, a charming word signifying a union, not cemented and unromanticized by documents.[114]

The War in Hollywood

DESTRY RIDES AGAIN 1939–1943

After two years without a film offer, any other actor would have been desperate for a chance to prove themselves, but not Dietrich. When she finally heard from Universal Studios' new producer and great hope, Joe Pasternak, offering her the starring role in *Destry Rides Again* (1939), she could hardly be bothered to reply, and, in true *Blue-Angel* manner, almost turned him down. If Hollywood had decided that she was box office poison, then there was no reason to submit herself to further humiliation. Universal Studios were the new kids on the block and nowhere near as powerful as MGM or Paramount Pictures. Even worse, Pasternak was asking her to star in a western, with the relatively unknown Jimmy Stewart – he would make his name later that year in *Mr Smith Goes to Washington* – and she was not even first choice (the studio wanted Paulette Goddard, but Pasternak insisted on Dietrich).

Dietrich finally agreed to take the part. She needed the money and, most of all, a film, to revive her stalled career. There were also possibilities of jobs for Sieber and Remarque through Universal Studios. Besides, now it was clear that Europe was no longer safe, they all needed to get back to America. Hitler and Goebbels had banned her films, but continued to send her invitations to return to the Third Reich; clearly, she needed to get herself, and her family, as far away from Germany as possible.

Dietrich left for the US on the S S *Normandie* at the end of August 1939. The remainder of her entourage, consisting of Sieber, Tami, Maria, their dog Teddy, and Remarque, sailed on the very last journey of HMS *Queen Mary* on 2 September; they had been at sea for

Destry Rides Again joined an astonishing string of classics, making 1939 the 'Golden Year' of Hollywood history

a day when Hitler marched into Poland, and Britain declared war on Germany.

To her surprise, Dietrich much enjoyed shooting *Destry Rides Again*. She received first billing, above Stewart, but with a relatively low salary of $75,000, was not the star, under pressure to carry the film. Her role was to entertain, to sing, fight and otherwise simply do her thing.

Destry Rides Again is loosely based on a Max Brand novel. The villains of Bottleneck, an archetypal, lawless, Western town, concoct a scheme to extort money from every passing cattle herder, fixing poker games, they cheat the local farmers out of their land until they control the whole valley. Thomas Jefferson Destry (James Stewart) the peace-loving deputy sheriff arrives and sorts out the villains, winning and losing Frenchy (Dietrich) in the meantime. The role of Frenchy was an addition to the original story; Dietrich has very little actually to do. To make sense of her presence, Pasternak hired *The Blue Angel*'s composer Friedrich Hollaender, aided by the American songwriter, Frank Loesser, to write her three songs. 'Li'l Joe Wrangler', 'You've Got That Look, That Look That Leaves Me Weak', and, 'See What the Boys in the Backroom Will Have' (which immediately became a standard in her repertoire). The songs tie together the narrative, making Frenchy the essential character and, in the words of the town-drunkard-cum-sheriff, Wash Dimsdale (Charles Winninger), '[Frenchy is] the real boss of Bottleneck.'

Despite Frenchy's dubious morality and character flaws, Dietrich makes her funny, and endearing, she is the only one to change, sacrificing her life to save Destry. A vivacious glamour takes the place of the burnished perfection as seen in her previous films. She lets herself be filmed, dirty and wet, and even did her own stunts. This was something new for Dietrich, and everyone – the public, the press, and the studio – loved it.

With *Destry Rides Again*, Dietrich achieved what became known as the biggest comeback in Hollywood history. Her reviews equalled those for her performance in *The Blue Angel*. She was glowing. Within a week of meeting her, James Stewart was in love. According to Maria, they conducted a passionate affair, which ended with Dietrich having an abortion.

JOINING THE WAR EFFORT

Dietrich was a sensation again, and Universal Studios happily allowed Joe Pasternak free rein to direct Dietrich in her next film, *Seven Sinners* (1940). As her leading man, Pasternak presented emerging star John Wayne. The two actors shared an agent, Charles Feldman, and Universal Studios bought them as a team. Wayne was good-looking, with the right hardness around the edges to provide the strength needed for wartime America. Wayne's wife claimed Dietrich initiated an affair immediately, but Maria insisted that it never happened, despite her mother's frequent attempts. Whatever the

Marlene Dietrich and John Wayne in *Seven Sinners* (1940). Dietrich loved suits and uniforms; they made dressing easy and gender a mystery

truth, Dietrich was piqued enough to describe Wayne as *not a bright or exciting type. He confessed to me that he never read books. But that didn't prevent him from accumulating a nice pile of money over the years. It proves that you don't have to be terribly brilliant to become a great film star.*[115] Their films were successful; their polarized acting styles, complemented each other and provided great screen chemistry. In the early 1940s, she enjoyed working on their movies, and bringing beef tea to his dressing room.

Dietrich had always felt alienated in the USA and, whenever there, needed Maria for support. But in the 1940s with a growing number of exiles arriving in Hollywood; the old Europe she had been missing was coming to her. She was suddenly the touchstone for a disappearing world, the interpreter of America for the refugees. Her dependence on Maria lessened as Dietrich found herself in the thick of one of the most energetic and creative periods in her life; her career was back on track and she once again fêted by Hollywood, and her many lovers. She needed no one's help or guidance, she now had what she had always wanted, the best of both worlds.

Almost immediately after their arrival, Dietrich sent Sieber off to New York City, to work as foreign-language dubber for Universal Studios' East Coast office. She also began to push Remarque in the direction of New York. Brooding in Hollywood, he had turned into a jealous nuisance rather than a pleasant diversion. Immersed in depression, he was writing a new novel, *Arch of Triumph* (1946), inspired by their affair. By the time it was complete they were no longer lovers. Set in 1939, the book tells the story of a German refugee physician in Paris, who makes his living treating the upper classes, whilst trying to track down the Nazis who tortured him. He falls for an actress, Joan Madou. The novel was another success for Remarque; it sold two million copies in the USA alone. Dietrich laughed when she read it in Paris after the war. In a letter to Sieber she wrote: *The love scenes are literature and boring – but it is a good film story with action once it gets started. He paints me worse than I am in order to make himself more interesting, and he succeeds. I am much more interesting than Joan Madou.*[116] Remarque married Paulette Goddard in 1958; until then he continued to escort Dietrich whenever they encountered each other.

After *Destry Rides Again* and the outbreak of war in Europe, cinema became of secondary importance to Dietrich. Although, with her career in the ascendent, she could enjoy living the Hollywood highlife. The constant flood of émigrés brought the horrors of the war in her native Germany unbearably close. Unable to contact anyone within Nazi Germany, she kept her radio tuned constantly to the European news and she cursed America's indifference to the war. She applauded when they finally joined Britain against Germany and Japan after the bombing of Pearl Harbor in December 1941.

Like many other exiles, Dietrich threw herself into the war effort with a gritty determination. She sold war bonds by touring nightclubs, singing on the radio, and selling kisses; she would do anything to promote the cause. Eventually President Roosevelt had to douse her enthusiasm, for in spite of her good intentions and initiative in raising funds for the armed forces, he was uncomfortable with her methods .

As the stories of the concentration camps and the full horrors of the Nazi regime began to cross the ocean, Dietrich was convinced that supporting the Allies was the right thing to do. But she was torn by guilt as she collected the money, which would help bomber

WORLD WAR II

1939: Germany annexes Czechoslovakia and invades Poland. 3 September, Britain and France declare war on Germany.

1939: General Franco becomes dictator of Spain.

1940: Germany occupies Denmark and Norway in April, and France, Belgium, and the Netherlands in May. The Blitz; Hitler tries to bomb England into submission with continuing air raids against London. Italy joins with Germany. Australia prepares for an invasion by Japan.

1941: Allies overrun Italy's African colonies. Germany arrives in Libya to help Italy. In December, Japan takes over French colonies in Southeast Asia and attack US pacific fleet at Pearl Harbor, Hawaii. The USA joins the war with the Allies against Germany. German troops take over Hungary, Bulgaria, Greece, and parts of Yugoslavia.

1941–42: Japan captures Hong Kong, Malaya, Philippines, Singapore, Indonesia, and Burma.

1942: German troops land in Morocco. The US Navy defeats Japan in Coral Sea off New Guinea and at Midway Island.

1943: American victories against Japan, and Allies invade Italy.

1943–44: The Germans are driven out of Russia.

1944: Japan attacks India but is defeated at Kohima. The Allies invade France and drive back the Germans.

1945: 7 May Germany surrenders. After tests in New Mexico, the US drops two atomic bombs on Hiroshima and Nagasaki on 6 August and 9 August. Japan surrenders on 14 August. World War II ends.

planes reduce her beloved country to rubble, and perhaps kill her mother, her family and friends who remained in Germany.

She worked with Ernst Lubitsch and Billy Wilder (by now in the USA) to set up the Hollywood Committee in an attempt to bring refugees out of Germany and soon much of the rest of Europe. She vouched for visa-seeking immigrants, gave them money and food when they arrived, and, whenever possible, used her connections to find them employment.

With the excuse of protecting 'the child's innocence' on their return to Hollywood, Dietrich installed Maria, now 17 years old, with a governess in her own private apartments. Maria was getting steadily heavier, eventually reaching over 14 stone, and her mother showed little sympathy. Maria said years later – after she had married, lost weight, and had children of her own – in a 1951 interview with *Ladies Home Journal*, 'I was always self-conscious because of my mother's beauty. She was so beautiful that it always gave me a feeling of ugliness and unworthiness. All my life I suffered because I was terribly overweight and I felt my mother [was] ashamed of me.

Marlene Dietrich with her daughter Maria at a CBS broadcast in 1943

I got fat because my childhood was miserable.'[117] Maria was abused by her live-in governess, and to escape the situation, she briefly got engaged to Richard Haydn (a 37-year-old British actor), when she turned 18 in December 1942. Dietrich, ignorant of the traumas in her daughter's life, sought to protect herself. Disapproving of the engagement, she comforted herself with a new lover.

Jean Gabin came to Hollywood in 1941. He was unlike any man Dietrich had known before. Free of intellectual pretension, Gabin was from provincial France, celebrated in his country as a man of the people. His personality was the complete opposite to Dietrich's. His straightforward acting had a visceral quality that made Dietrich lust for him. Gabin and Dietrich started what would become one of the most intense love affairs of both of their lives.

Aside from the confused flop, *The Flame of New Orleans* (1941) – a film Dietrich made as a favour to the newly-arrived French director, René Clair – her movies continued to be reflections of the ethos of the period; her role was than of an earthy vamp. Hollywood profited while increasing public support for the war, making a series of films on heroic themes, usually on the subject of the common man standing up to the evils of corruption. The message could hardly have been clearer: young men were leaving their country once more, to lay down their lives – they needed to believe they were dying for a just cause. The role of women in these films was relegated to one of support or passivity; they were there to help their men through the struggle. The independence of the thirties woman was replaced with self-negating love of male authority. Dietrich's feelings on this were equivocal; she lived her adult life by the rules of a Weimar Woman, but had always treated male authority figures with the greatest respect. For example, whilst having one affair after another, she had never stopped loving her husband and she never publicly humiliated or contradicted him. In fact, she actively sought his opinion and followed his advice. She was comfortable playing women in a wartime role and, even when the films flopped, the critics commended her acting.

In *Seven Sinners* (1940) Dietrich plays Bijou, a cabaret singer (and loose woman) who knows that her potentially evil character will destroy the future of her love. Unlike Amy Jolie in *Morocco*, a decade earlier, Bijou lets her Navy officer, John Wayne go off to fight, alone. (The film added a couple of new Hollaender songs to her repertoire: 'The Man's in the Navy', 'I've Been in Love Before', 'I Fall Overboard'.)

Manpower (1941) has Dietrich, once more playing a loose woman, marrying a decent man, but actually loving his best friend; she eventually causes her husband's death as the two friends fight over her.

In 1941, she also appeared in Columbia's *The Lady Is Willing*. In this rather offensive morality tale, women are reminded of the value of motherhood. Elizabeth Madden (Dietrich), a successful and wealthy singer, is ridiculed when she adopts a baby but does not know what to do with it. It takes the love of a man to show her the way to happiness, found ultimately in maternal love and marriage.

Midway through the film, Dietrich fell while holding the baby. As a mother herself, she automatically twisted her body to protect him and broke her ankle.

She received much publicity and consequently, public praise through the accident, but it precipitated an extreme superstition which lasted to the end of her life. Her astrologer, Carrol Righter had warned her, that morning, of an impending accident. From that moment Righter was consulted on every decision (unless, of course, it was too inconvenient). He made charts for her, her family, her friends, as well as her lovers.

After only four days away from the set, Dietrich returned with what was then still a novelty, a walking cast. This was a wonderful opportunity for publicity, but with the restricted movement, she needed to practise to appear natural on the screen. Herbert Marshall (her screen husband in *Blonde Venus*), who had lost a leg in World War I, had acted with a prosthetic limb for years. She rented his films and watched them until she had learned his tricks.

Back at Universal Studios in 1942, John Wayne joined Dietrich in two films: *The Spoilers,* a tale of 'gold and greed';[118] and *Pittsburgh,* a classic story of male rivalry. In both films, she is in love with an unworthy man, who has to prove himself deserving.

In 1942, Maria enrolled at the newly established Max Reinhardt Academy in Hollywood, much to her mother's pleasure, to train as an actress. Dietrich liked the idea of closing of the circle that this enrolment implied. Having heard the lie so often, everyone believed she was a past Reinhardt student; now her daughter was one as well. Maria's teacher was Reinhardt's wife Helene Thimig (unemployed like many exiled German actresses who could only find work playing the Nazi enemy). Maria was taught stage craft and given two years of intensive education. She had talent and excelled. When the Reinhardt school, with its rigid German stage techniques, failed and was taken over by the Geller Workshop – a talent-shaping acting school better suited to Hollywood's less formal requirements – Maria stayed on as a teacher, an impressive feat for one so young. Calling herself Maria Manton, she had the same reddish-blonde hair, blue eyes, and fine complexion as her mother. She carried herself with style and authority although she was only 18, but was seen by some as aloof.

As the enlistment intensified, so did Hollywood's participation in the war. Dietrich joined other stars entertaining recruits at the Hollywood Canteen. Before going off to the war, the conscripts, many barely Maria's age, would be served sandwiches by the stars and have the chance to dance with the screen goddesses. Dietrich danced, washed the dishes in the kitchen, handed them food; she could have been the mother of these boys and she loved every moment of it.

As a tribute to the American Forces, Hollywood put together an all-star musical package, *Follow the Boys* (1944) (originally called *Three Cheers for the Boys).* Dietrich assisted her good friend and admirer, Orson Welles (1915–85), in his show, helping him with his magic tricks, mind-reading and being sawn in half. He had been performing for the servicemen for a while, but when his most recent

Rita Hayworth, Orson Welles and Marlene Dietrich enjoying a wartime cup of coffee. *When I have seen [Welles] and talked with him, I feel like a plant that has been watered.* MARLENE DIETRICH [119]

wife, Rita Hayworth, was prevented by Columbia Pictures from assisting him in a Universal Studios film, he recruited Dietrich. Gabin paced the wings jealously, but although Dietrich adored Welles's genius, as she did Hemingway's, he was never more than a close friend to her.

On 23 August 1943, in the presence of just a few witnesses, Maria married a 23-year-old fellow Geller Workshop actor, Dean Truman Goodman after a seven-week courtship. Her parents disapproved and did not attend. Dietrich, panicked, trying to stop Maria's hasty decision. She had Goodman investigated in an attempt to find a reason against the marriage, but Maria was not to be dissuaded. She needed to escape both her mother and her governess; anyone who would have her and who would love her would suffice. Dietrich declared that she would not help the couple financially, but in the end she did, making it possible for them to rent and furnish an apartment in Westwood. Goodman and Maria separated within three months. Goodman, upon returning from a theatre tour, found himself without his wife. He had never met his parents-in-law. Maria returned home, chastened, and needing her mother again.

At the time, Dietrich was renting a simple house in Brentwood and welcomed Maria back into her life. But Maria had to compete with Jean Gabin for her mother's affections. Gabin's film was going badly and he was growing restless and jealous. Dietrich told Gabin she loved only him, but the many ghosts from her past were creating problems; love-letters had a habit of emerging among her correspondence. They fought frequently, but though they always made up, their relationship was deteriorating. A home-movie from this time shows them in the early morning gazing lovingly into each other's eyes, but frustration is written all over Gabin's face; the hedonistic lifestyle of Hollywood infuriated him. He was riven by guilt knowing that his family, friends, and, countrymen, were at war while he lived in sybaritic exile. By the end of 1943, Gabin had had enough of Hollywood and left to train as a tank commander for the Free French Forces. Dietrich was heartbroken and feebly begged him to stay. To be with him just a bit longer, she confronted her fear of flying and flew to New York to spend a last few days with him before he left for Europe.

With Gabin gone, and her films resorting to cliché, Dietrich saw little point in remaining. Many Hollywood actors had already left to serve their various countries. An American citizen since 1939, she enlisted with the USO and the Office of Strategic Services (later CIA), hoping to support the American war effort.

Waiting to be granted her clearance to join the Americans in Europe, she signed up for *Kismet* (1943) at MGM. She was to be directed by Wilhelm Dieterle, who she had worked with in Germany on *Der Mensch am Wege* (*Man by the Wayside*, 1923).

To her relief, the resulting film, *Kismet*, was one of her greatest hits. A remake of the celebrated play by Edward Knobloch, it was a grand spectacle woven around a fairy-tale theme, but seems rather slow by today's standards. The cinematographer, art director, set designer, and sound recordist were all nominated for Academy Awards. Dietrich, hoping to replicate the power of the image that von Sternberg had created for her in *The Devil is a Woman*, took control of her lighting and costumes, with the help of Maria, and dress designers Irene (Lenz-Gibbons, 1901–62) and Karinska.

Assisted by Irene, she invented her own foundation garment. This gave the illusion of a perfect body shape. Now that she had passed forty, and was worried about her increasing number of wrinkles, she pulled back her hair under wigs, creating an instant and painful face-lift. Dietrich's coiffures by Sidney Guilleroff and the variety of glorious costumes were made a lasting impression on cinema audiences. That she was in pain, with a bleeding scalp and restricted movement was unnoticeable. To distract from her impaired mobility, she designed costume of chains, but had to abandon the idea because of the noise they made. As an alternative she painted her legs with gold. The paint almost gave her lead poisoning, and she was soon dizzy from the fumes. The press loved it.

By the time of *Kismet* completion, close to Christmas 1943, the

FBI had concluded their background security check and confirmed that Dietrich was a loyal American citizen. She was reported to have owned a safety deposit box and had had relationships with notorious lesbians, but there was no reason to believe that she had ever engaged in any espionage. Her enthusiastic participation in the selling of war bonds had assisted her application. She went to war as part of the American army.

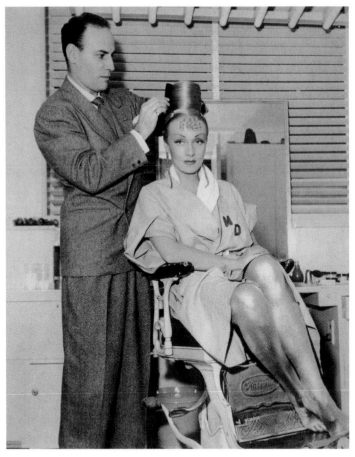

Dietrich and Guilleroff on the set of *Kismet*, 1943

INVESTIGATED

If you haven't been in the war, don't talk about it.[120]

An Officer's Daughter

AT THE FRONT 1944–1945

For a decade, Dietrich had been aware of the threat posed by the Nazis in Germany. By the autumn of 1932, Sieber advised her not to return to Berlin on holiday. He feared a civil war, and was afraid that she might be prevented from leaving the country. Dietrich and Sieber knew the film industry in Germany and saw the effects of Hitler's Aryan laws. Dietrich's nostalgia for the Germany of her childhood, for the Weimar years, remained with her always and she saw it as a personal insult that her own country was now endeavouring to destroy everything in which she believed.

To give up your homeland and mother tongue, even when forced to it by circumstance, is an almost unendurable ordeal. Only German, this lovely language, has remained to me as a legacy. I came very close to forgetting it the more securely I settled in America and felt sufficiently at home in English.[121]

She relished the image of herself as a soldier's daughter; and saw her time entertaining the US military as the most meaningful role she ever undertook.

Preparations for her USO shows began in New York in early 1944 where she met a young comedian from Chicago, Danny Thomas. Dietrich had last been on stage, in Berlin, a decade and a half earlier, performing in German; she had no experience of the type of audience that waited for her at the front. And though Thomas left the show after only six weeks, his advice would provide the basis for all Dietrich's future stage work. Years later she wrote, *Danny taught me how to keep my self-control, how to impose silence on the audience. He also taught me a flair for timing, how to get a laugh, and how to stop one, and how to handle all those desperate kids who wanted to humiliate anyone who hadn't been in combat. This hostility was the most difficult to overcome.*[122]

Marlene Dietrich playing the Musical Saw

On 14 April 1944, she flew out of New York via Greenland and the Azores, to Casablanca and Algiers. Dietrich's wartime shows played on sexual innuendo; they consisted of a mind-reading act which began with a line, directed to the whole audience, *When a GI looks at me, it's not hard to read his mind.*[123] This could have summed up the entire show and the GIs loved her. She performed in an Irene-designed gold-sequinned dress so sheer it gave the impression of shimmering nudity. Sometimes she would start the show by simply extending a bare leg through the curtain.

Dietrich finished by playing her Musical Saw, with her dress hiked up, revealing her legs. She sang her old hit songs like 'See What the Boys in the Backroom Will Have' and soon added 'Lili Marleen' to her repertoire. This song would in time become completely hers.

She loved all the attention, she let 'her boys' crowd around her, touch her, talk with her, have their picture taken with her arms around them and occasionally even kiss her. She encouraged, loved, comforted, and joked with them, she made a real difference to many thousands of soldiers. She saw her job there as being to improve morale, to send frightened young boys into battle feeling like brave soldiers, and she took her mission very seriously. She could have died from pneumonia in Italy in 1944, had she not been cured by the newly available penicillin. (After the war, she was able to thank Alexander Fleming, sending him gifts. By way of a response, he sent her a sample of the original *penicillium notatum* culture.)

Dietrich toured through North Africa, Italy, and France. She managed to meet up with Jean Gabin for a momentary embrace, when she learned that Free French troops were at the front. She was close enough to the Battle of the Bulge to feel the effect of the exploding shells.

By the time the war was nearing its end, she had attached herself to General George Patton's Third Army. As Patton raced into

---

'Lili Marleen' was loved by soldiers of both sides in WWII. Hans Leip wrote the lyrics during WWI, combining the names of a girlfriend and a nurse; Norbert Schultze set it to music in 1938, and the German actress, Lale Andersen recorded it just before WWI. Dietrich sang it for the American GIs and went on featuring it for the remainder of her career.

Lili Marleen

Outside the barracks, by the corner light
I'll always stand and wait for you at night
We will create a world for two
I'd wait for you, the whole night through
For you, Lili Marleen; For you, Lili Marleen.

Bugler, tonight don't play the call to arms
I want another evening with her charms
Then we will say goodbye and part.
I'll always keep you in my heart
With me, Lili Marleen; With me, Lili Marleen.

Give me a rose to show how much you care
Tie to the stem a lock of golden hair
Surely tomorrow you'll feel blue
But then will come a love that's new
For you, Lili Marleen; For you, Lili Marleen.

When we are marching in the mud and cold
And when my pack seems more than I can hold
My love for you renews my might
I'm warm again, my pack is light,
It's you Lili Marleen; It's you Lili Marleen.

Marlene Dietrich entertaining the American GIs at Caserta in Italy, 1944

Germany, concern was voiced for her safety. General Omar Bradley told her to remain behind, by order of the Allied Commander-in-Chief, Dwight D Eisenhower. No doubt the flamboyant Patton was thrilled at having her along and General Bradley was probably glad to be rid of her; he gave her two bodyguards and she entered Germany in the forward columns of the US Army.

This was her first time in Germany since 1931 and she was now, entering as an American citizen. If she was apprehensive, she need not have been. The people welcomed her back with open arms.

As the Allies uncovered the unbelievable horrors of the concentration camps, Dietrich worried more and more about her mother and sister. The Nazis had punished families for far less

THE GENERALS

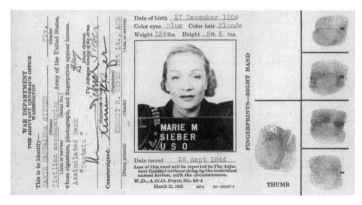

Dietrich's military identification card, 1944

an offence than having a relative serving in the enemy army and Berlin had endured terrible bombing raids in recent months.

In February 1945 Dietrich was sent back to Paris with frostbite and the flu. There she performed at the French equivalent of the Hollywood Canteen with Noël Coward and Maurice Chevalier, who was being investigated for collaboration. Dietrich embraced him saying, *No one believes the stories, no one who knows you.*[125]

There are several versions of the war-time fate of Dietrich's sister Liesel and of how the two were reunited. For a while, it was feared that Liesel and her family were in fact prisoners at the Bergen-Belsen concentration camp. In fact Georg Will, Liesel's husband, ran a cinema in Belsen, which had been frequented by the Nazi personnel from the camp.

Dietrich awkwardly refused to discuss her sister and never excused or condemned her. Later on, if the topic of Liesel arose, she kept the legend of her supposed imprisonment alive by simply saying that she was 'in Belsen' during the war, letting the listeners draw their own conclusions, hoping one day she might come to believe this herself. In later years when they saw each other, they would travel quietly in England or Switzerland. In Maximilian Schell's documentary, *Marlene* (1984), Dietrich insists that she has no sister (Liesel was, in fact, dead by then) and when she published her childhood photographs in a book, she cut her sister out of the pictures. The matter of the Wills' wartime occupation might have embarrassed her later on, but in 1945 she was just another relative desperate to be reunited with her sister. She vouched for the family to the occupying British Army, and the Will family were allowed to keep the cinema, which they certainly would have lost otherwise.

The Russians had taken Berlin and, until the American forces reached the city, Dietrich had no news of her mother. When at last on 1 July 1945 the Americans entered her home town, she requested help to find her mother, Josefine von Losch, from every general that she met. Col Barney Oldfield and Lt Col Albert McCleery, serving under Dietrich's personal friend Lt General James M Gavin, the 82nd Airborne Division's commander, were the first to find Josefine. She had moved, because of bomb damage, and was caring for a 95-year-old aunt and, although hungry, was quite well. Dietrich was contacted in Paris with the news. The first telephone conversation between mother and daughter, on the army's radio, is recorded. Dietrich had not spoken to, or heard from her mother for six years and, for security reasons, they were forced to speak in English. They had about two minutes to exchange all they were longing to say. The emotional tone of the exchange encapsulates the horrors of war and separation.

MD: *Mami, we have to speak English.*

JvL: Yes. Lena, my lovely Lena, I am so glad to hear your voice.

MD: *Mami, Liesel and the son are fine.*

JvL: You saw Liesel?

MD: *Yes, she is fine.*

JvL: Lena, I am so glad and thankful for all that you have done.

MD: *Mami, you suffered for my sake, I am so sorry, forgive me.*

JvL: Yes, my love.

MD: *I am coming soon.*

JvL: Goodbye, mein Herz.

MD: *Goodbye Mami.* [126]

Almost immediately, Dietrich was flown out to Berlin on a

The American Army organized for Josefine von Losch to welcome her daughter home at the Tempelhof Airport, Berlin, 1945

military transport. Col Barney Oldfield arranged for Josefine and a photographer to meet the plane on the tarmac. One of many wartime reunions became a perfect photo opportunity. Josefine was proud and happy to see her daughter. Dietrich was proven right; her mother had wanted her to fight.

Many of her friends had left Berlin in 1933. She walked the streets, happy to be home, listening to Berliner voices and bewailing the destruction of her city. The apartment building she and Sieber had lived in had survived, but her mother's home had been destroyed completely, and she had lost many of her belongings. Meanwhile, in the Russian-controlled section of Czechoslovakia, the house of Sieber's parents had been destroyed and they had been placed in a refugee camp. Dietrich travelled half the country to bring them to Berlin, but found when she reached the camp that, desperate and starving, they had already left on foot for her mother's house. She used her connections with Lt General Gavin to get them permission to stay in Berlin, and got them ration books and an apartment.

Dietrich went back to New York, giving up her guns at customs. She was suddenly a civilian again and at a loss. In addition, she discovered that she was completely broke. For once Sieber was the breadwinner, but he could never provide enough for a star's needs.

Maria, who had just closed a play, *Foolish Notion*, on Broadway, signed on with USO to act for the many troops still in service in Europe and Asia. Dietrich flew back to Jean Gabin in Paris and the happy prospect of making a film together.

Having seen Hitler defeated, Josefine died on 6 November 1945. Dietrich used her military connections to get word to Maria, who was with the USO in Stuttgart, and turned to General Gavin for help. The army was not meant to fraternize with the defeated enemy, so there could be no official involvement in the arrangements of Josefine's funeral. Without giving a direct order, General Gavin sent Col Barney Oldfield. He organised four paratroopers of the 82nd Airborne Division to dig the grave and found a German undertaker willing to perform the ceremony. In the middle of the night, they took Josefine's coffin from her house and, in Dietrich's presence, performed an *ad hoc* funeral, after which the paratroopers filled in the grave. Dietrich was eternally grateful to General Gavin and the 82nd Airborne Division. Maria, having left in the middle of her show, did not make it in time for the funeral.

Thanksgiving, 1945 [to Maria]

Mein Engel, I wanted to talk to you so badly. And be with you. If you could only get out of the show and live with me. I need your advice for so many things . . . and wish you were here to help me make order in my head and heart. All my love, Angel Face. You are so wonderful inside and outside – and quite apart from my mother-love I love you terribly. Mammi [127]

The two missed each other in Berlin. In between running affairs with both Jean Gabin and General Gavin, Dietrich was desperately lonely and longed for her daughter. She wrote her long letters from Paris, disregarding any independence her daughter might have found.

The war left Dietrich without a country, with her mother dead and her sister married to a probable Nazi collaborator; she was virtually without family or friends in Germany. Maria became even more important in Dietrich's life. Her days of rebellion and her teenage marriage were in the past. Once more, she became the foundation of Dietrich's life. From then on, Maria was Dietrich's sole confidant and her mother's secrets and fears took precedence over her own problems and needs.

I started smoking during the war. I have kept it up ever since. It keeps me healthy.[128]

Post-War Depression

Dietrich had no place in the army after the end of war. The large crowds of adoring young boys were gone, she had no show to perform, and could no longer travel around in uniform, but had to think about hats, shoes, and gloves again. The Europe she had known was shattered and the Germany she had loved no longer existed.

Soon letters from 'her boys' began to reach the various war departments around the world; all claiming that Dietrich had made more of a difference to the war effort than any other entertainer. She was decorated by France, Belgium, Israel, and the USA. She was the first woman to receive the US government's Medal of Freedom. France honoured her with three degrees of the Légion D'Honneur during her lifetime. She had made something of herself and knew that her parents would have been proud.

Dietrich and Gabin were in France to make the eagerly awaited *Martin Roumagnac* (1946). Gabin was a national hero and this was his first French film since his exile to the US, so he could not afford a failure. But this cumbersome film, is ill-served by mediocre performances from both Gabin and Dietrich. Martin Roumagnac (Gabin) falls in love with prostitute Blanche Ferrand (Dietrich), only to kill her. At his trial he is acquitted on a technicality and a rejected suitor kills Roumagnac to avenge her. Shocked by the open depiction of prostitution, American censors cut almost thirty minutes from this film. In order to entice the audience, the title was changed to *The Room Upstairs.*

Jean Gabin's jealousy of Dietrich had intensified and he became

Dietrich in *Martin Roumagnac* with Jean Gabin: *Jean Gabin was the man, the superman, the 'man for life'. He was the ideal that all women seek. Nothing in him was false. Everything was clear and transparent. He was good and outdid those who vainly tried to do the same to him. But he was stubborn, extremely possessive and jealous. I like all these qualities about him, and we never seriously quarrelled.*[129]

violently paranoid. He wanted marriage and children, and finally started to have affairs himself. To make things worse, Dietrich and he were making a terrible film together, and they both knew it.

BACK TO HOLLYWOOD

With an offer of $100,000 from Mitchell Leisen (her old director from *The Lady Is Willing*), Dietrich left Gabin and Paris and returned to Hollywood to play a gypsy in *Golden Earrings* (1946), her first film back at Paramount Pictures. This was the opportunity she needed to restart her Hollywood career, and she needed the money.

Golden Earrings is light-hearted and fun, graced with an entertaining performance from Dietrich. She had seen gypsies in England, and her wardrobe assistant, Nellie, created a black wig; Maria was on hand as an assistant and as dialogue coach. Dietrich gives a passionate portrayal as one of the most glamorous gypsies in cinema history. She did not like her co-star, Ray Milland, and the feeling was mutual. She found him uptight and boring and tried her best to disgust him with her gypsy behaviour, sucking on fish eyes and rubbing her grimy body against his.

The film is set just before Britain enters the war. Col Ralph Denistoun (Milland) and a young officer, Byrd (Bruce Lester), are running from Nazi officials to reach the brilliant Professor Krosigk (Reinhold Schunzel) and take his poison gas formula out of the country. They are helped to escape by the Lydia, a gypsy (Dietrich). The knowledge that gypsies had been murdered in concentration camps provides an ominous undertone throughout the film.

Shooting time was pushed into 1947, as the production was briefly delayed by a union strike which forced everyone to stay on at the studio, sleeping on cots or in their dressing room. The critics hated *Golden Earrings*, but the film proved tremendously popular with audiences.

MASSY

On 4 July 1947, in New York, Maria married William Riva, a talented, young American-Italian scenic designer who loved her, and took no account of her famous mother. Dietrich was not at the wedding. Maria was teaching directing at Fordham University, alongside her new husband, and getting acting parts. Maria Sieber/Manton now became Maria Riva, beautiful, successful, the daughter that Dietrich had always wished for. What Maria wanted, however, was the one thing Dietrich had not given her – a large, loving family.

On 28 June 1948 Dietrich's first grandchild, John Michael Riva was born, putting Dietrich back in the headlines and on the cover of *Life* magazine as 'The World's Most Glamorous Grandmother.' The family nickname for Dietrich became 'Massy' from then

Marlene Dietrich's Famous Scrambled Eggs

3 eggs, 2 tablespoons mineral water, ¹/₂ teaspoon salt, a pinch of pepper, a pinch of thyme, 1 teaspoon freshly chopped parsley, 1 tablespoon freshly chopped chives, 2 tablespoons of cream, 200g (or more) butter. Mix the eggs with the water, salt, pepper, thyme and parsley. Add the cream. Allow the butter to melt in a hot pan before adding the egg. Leave for a moment before turning it, thereby creating large pieces. Cook for about five minutes. Serve with the browned butter from the pan and freshly chopped chives.[130]

onwards; her grandson's mispronunciation of her maid's 'Missy Dietrich'. Dietrich would eventually have three more grandsons. Her first great-grandchild, John Matthew Riva was born in 1976, the year Rudi Sieber and Jean Gabin died.

In 1951, her life insurance matured and she bought a $43,000 brownstone house on Manhattan for the Riva family on East 95th Street. As she still owned the house until it could legally be 'gifted' to her daughter, her control over Maria remained for many years .[131]

'PROSTITUTION'

With the war over, Dietrich began to regard her work on film as merely prostitution, to provide for her own expensive lifestyle and an increasing need to help her growing family.

Much against her better judgment, she was convinced by Billy Wilder to take the role of an ex-Nazi in *A Foreign Affair* (1948). She did the film out of her high regard and trust for him as an artist. Wilder had gone to Berlin immediately following the war to film in the destroyed city. Bomb craters, shattered buildings and the rubble of a destroyed Germany, served as the background for this comedy.

Captain Pringle (John Lund) loves an ex-Nazi, Erika von Schlütow (Dietrich). American officials, including Phoebe Frost (Jean Arthur), a conservative congresswoman from Iowa have come to investigate the morale of the US troops in Germany. Playing a nightclub singer, Dietrich sings 'Illusions', 'Black Market', and 'Ruins in Berlin', written and accompanied by Frederick Hollaender at the piano. Wilder's choice of ending has Captain Pringle choosing Phoebe over Erika, but would any man really have chosen Arthur over Dietrich?

Dietrich was praised by the critics; she gives a commendable performance, revealing a real sympathy for her character, but the film itself received mixed reviews. It was still too early to joke about a tragedy of this magnitude. The US military in Germany banned the picture.

In between films, regular radio performances on a Sunday show

Dietrich with Frederick Hollaender at the piano in *A Foreign Affair*, 1948

Hitchcock directs Dietrich and Hector McGregor in *Stage Fright* (1949)

called *Café Istanbul*, and a quick cameo in the independent film, *Jigsaw* (1949), Dietrich played loving grandmother to her grandson, Michael. She dressed herself in a nurse's uniform from Bloomingdales and strolled with his push-chair through Central Park. In between these familial duties, she conducted an affair with the publisher of *Vogue* magazine, I V A Patchevich, who installed her in a suite at the New York Plaza Hotel.

Her ever-trusted trusted agent, Charles Feldman secured a deal for the role of Charlotte Inwood, an actress, in Alfred Hitchcock's *Stage Fright* (1949). Contrary to his usual practise of demanding complete control, Hitchcock let Dietrich partially direct her own role and invited her to create her character's wardrobe with the assistance of a designer of her choosing. Dietrich chose Christian Dior, the post-war designer of the 'New Look', which she and Maria had worn for *Vogue* in 1947. She worked closely with the house, mixing and matching styles, to create the timeless look used in the film. Dior received the screen credit for the costumes.

Although this is one of Hitchcock's less successful films, it still has many of his distinctive touches. The cast includes Jane Wyman, who plays Eva Gill, Richard Todd, who plays her childhood sweetheart Jonathan Cooper, and Michael Wilding as the detective investigating a murder case in which Cooper's lover, Charlotte Inwood (Dietrich), is mysteriously involved. Dietrich, once again playing an entertainer, sings Cole Porter's 'The Laziest Girl in Town', and with the permission of her friend, Edith Piaf, 'La Vie en Rose'.

Alfred Hitchcock (1899–1980), English director, was known as 'The Master of Suspence'. Hitchcock was obviously greatly inspired by von Sternberg's films, both in the way he 'used' and 'portrayed' his women and in his love for the 'speaking' and 'floating' camera. In *Stage Fright*, he wanted von Sternberg's 'Marlene Dietrich' and he got her. He later called her the absolute professional, a professional actress, a professional wardrober, a professional director, and a professional lighting technician.

Audiences did not like the film feeling confused by the many twists and turns of the plot, that are left unresolved at the end. The audience is tricked, with a flashback, into believing that Charlotte had murdered her husband. (It was unprecedented for the time to lie in flashbacks, and the audience felt betrayed.) At the climax, Charlotte is not revealed as either innocent or guilty and the mystery is left unresolved. Those expecting fireworks from a Hitchcock/ Dietrich collaboration were left disappointed.

Dietrich and Wilding began an affair punctuated by his brief marriage to Elizabeth Taylor. Dietrich, about to become a grandmother for the second time, was invited to present the 1950 Academy Award for Best Foreign Film. She had not been nominated herself since her role in *Morocco*, but she decided there were other ways to steal the show. In striking contrast to other stars in their post-war frills and chiffon, she wore a slinky black dress, slit to reveal her entire leg as she walked to the podium. She was given a standing ovation in acknowledgement of her status, effectively stealing the thunder of every Oscar-winner that night.

As Maria's family grew larger, she needed Dietrich's help more and more. Tensions re-emerged between mother and daughter. Bitter letters, telegrams, and telephone calls flew between them. Maria could not avoid her mother's interference in her own life, but she was determined to protect her children from Dietrich's meddling.

With her own career in a slump, Dietrich did her very best to run Maria's developing career on live television. She would attend the rehearsals, demanding changes to Maria's lighting, hair, and make-up; once again overwhelming her daughter with her presence. In 1952 Dietrich and Maria were the subject of a feature article in *Life* magazine and were photographed together for the cover. Though it seemed a breakthrough for Maria, she would always be the daughter of Marlene Dietrich. In 1956 she retired from acting permanently to become a full-time mother.

In the early 1950s, recovering from surgery, Sieber bought a farm in California's San Fernando Valley, with a loan from a banker friend, Hans Kohn, (which Dietrich later paid off). He still loved Dietrich, but as the years passed he had come to appreciate Tami more.

Dietrich, feeling rejected by her family, and still missing the adoration of the thousands of admiring GIs, surrounded herself with lovers. In 1951 she became madly infatuated with Yul Brynner, the star of the Broadway hit, *The King and I*. Their affair lasted for four years.

No Highway [in the Sky] (1950) was shot in England and paired her for the second time with Jimmy Stewart. The film bored her and – their affair very much a thing of the past – so did he. Set on a aeroplane, the film has her playing a movie star. The role required little effort; the reviews matched her lack of interest.

Following this, Fritz Lang, her erstwhile lover and friend, directed her in *Rancho Notorious* (1952), a farrago of a film. It is not saved by Dietrich's entertaining imitation of her old Paramount friend, Mae West. Lang and Dietrich quarrelled throughout the production. On a promotional tour for the film, paid $5,000 a night, Dietrich was intrigued to discover that, although the audience might not flock to see her films, they did come to see her in person.

Dietrich with Arthur Kennedy (*left*) and Mel Ferrer (*right*) in
Rancho Notorious, 1952

Ideals are the best food for stamina and superhuman endurance.[132]

The Stage

In the 1950s a new generation of younger actresses was getting the starring roles. The ideal screen image for a woman had changed from mysterious temptress to the girl next door. Dietrich transformed herself from screen goddess to movie legend.

Without film offers, Dietrich agreed to help out at one of Maria's (and Yul Brynner's) favourite charity events, raising funds and awareness for Children with Cerebral Palsy. At a fundraiser at Madison Square Garden, celebrities became circus performers for the night. Dietrich, never a team-player, agreed to act as the ring-mistress. She arrived in small black shorts, top-hat and, of course, a whip. She stole the show and photographs were featured in *Vogue* and every newspaper.

In the summer of 1953, Dietrich was offered $20,000 from *Ladies Home Journal* to write a feature on 'How to be Loved', and a contract from the publishers Doubleday to write a short book on *Beauty and Love*, receiving a $10,000 advance. (She failed to meet the contract and the advance was returned.) Even more tempting – and remunerative – was on offer from The Sahara in Las Vegas to appear for three weeks over Christmas 1953, for a fee of $30,000 a week, the highest price ever paid to a Las Vegas entertainer at that time. It was an offer she could not refuse. But she needed to create a style for the stage similar to the one that she had perfected on screen. *I needed costumes,* she explained, *as I had no illusions about my voice.*[133]

What she wanted to take with her was the stylish glamour of a movie star; and she knew that only a film studio could provide it. Serendipitously, Harry Cohn, the Head of Columbia Pictures,

Dietrich in her ring-mistress costume designed by Jean Louis
(Berthault, 1907–97), 1953

wanted her to play a part in the movie *Pal Joey,* and so allowed her
to work with a favourite designer, Jean Louis. Cohn joined her list
of lovers, but this didn't stop her refusing a part in the film. He
threw her off the Columbia lot as a result, but she was back working
with Jean Louis almost immediately. Dietrich had a unique way of
persuading men to grant the favours she needed.

The 'Eel Dress' by Jean Louis

Jean Louis and Dietrich spent thousands of dollars – and nearly as many hours – creating what Dietrich would later describe as, *works of art*.[134] Some of these stupendous creations are now on display at the Film Museum in Berlin, bearing witness to her legendary stage performances. Her shimmering dresses were reworked versions of her wartime costumes, giving the illusion of a perfectly-formed nude figure untouched by age. She wrapped herself in fur, feathers, chiffon, beads, rhinestones – any effect that would dazzle her audience.

Singing the songs she had collected over her thirty-year career, she added a few new ones at Maria's suggestion, such as, 'Where Have All the Flowers Gone' and 'Whoopee'. Audiences came from all over the world to see the legend for themselves.

She signed a multi-year Las Vegas contract, and following her first engagements, an offer from Major Neville Wilding brought her to the Café de Paris in London for a four-week contract. He had promised that each night, at midnight, a famous actor would introduce her show. On the opening night, Noël Coward began a long line of tributes with a poem. She took London by storm.

Following Dietrich's successes in Las Vegas and London she would go on to tour the world with a one-woman show at the beginning of the 1960s. But in the mid-1950s, she was still shuttling between Las Vegas and London, visiting few other places. Between engagements, she spent time in California with Sieber and saw her grandchildren as often as she could. The Rivas had settled in London for the sake of the children's schooling as they later would in Switzerland. To

Marlene Dietrich with her great friend and confidant Noël Coward. When passing each other in various cities they would always see each other off at the airport

be close to them, Dietrich took an apartment in Paris, on Avenue Montaigne, opposite the Plaza Athénée and alternated between there and her Park Avenue apartment in Manhattan. This arrangement continued until she settled permanently in Paris in the late 1970s.

With a new and adoring audience, and once more earning sufficient income to satisfy her extravagant needs, Dietrich's self-assurance was back.

'We know God made the trees / And the birds and the bees / And seas, for the fishes to swim in / We are also aware / That he had quite a flair / For creating exceptional women . . . / Now we all might enjoy / Seeing Helen of Troy / As a gay cabaret entertainer / But I doubt that she could / Be one quarter as good / As our legend'ry, lovely Marlene!'
NOËL COWARD [135]

In 1956, Dietrich was back in Hollywood for a cameo in *Around the World in 80 days* (1956) produced by Michael Todd for United Artists, with about 40 other stars ranging from Sir John Gielgud to Noël Coward, Buster Keaton, Trevor Howard, Peter Lorre, Cesar Romero, John Mills, Shirley MacLaine, and Frank Sinatra.

The film was a triumph, and won five Academy Awards, including Best Picture. Any suspicions that Dietrich had lost her screen magnetism were allayed; United Artist offered her a part in an Italian co-production, *The Monte Carlo Story* (1957).

Whilst her affair with Yul Brynner continued through most of the 1950s, she was apparently also involved with the composer Harold Arlen, as well as Kirk Douglas, Michael Wilding, Frank Sinatra, Edith Piaf, the American Ambassador to the United Nations, Adlai E Stevenson, the Hollywood producers Sam Spiegel and Michael Todd, and the news reporter and war correspondent, Edward E Murrow, to name but a few.

In 1957, Dietrich lobbied for the role of Christine Vole in Billy Wilder's *Witness for the Prosecution* (1957). An adaptation from an Agatha Christie play, most of the story takes place in a courtroom in London's Old Bailey – re-created on a Hollywood soundstage and populated with American extras.

Although this was the first time that Dietrich had taken a character role, her work is immaculate; she is imperious as Mrs Vole and shrew-like when disguised as the cockney girl. Charles Laughton and Nöel Coward had taught her to speak with a convincing East London accent.

Dietrich was well aware that few thought of her as an actress capable of caring for anything beyond her looks. But although she sat in silence while Laughton and Wilder discussed her scenes, her comments on her character and the production were astute. In a letter to Maria, she could not refrain from questioning her director and co-star's reluctance to listen to her input. *I have played whores all my life. And this one they don't even think I can contribute anything to. Whereas Mrs Vole, a character I have never played before, they thought (up to the time Laughton got his fingers into it) perfectly played . . .*[136]

Critics thought Dietrich had finally showed some depth of talent. Yet many suspected that the cockney voice had been dubbed; though this was not true, the doubts kept her from being nominated for one of the five Academy Awards the film would receive (including Best Picture, Best Supporting Actress, Best Actor for Laughton, and Best Director for Wilder). Laughton praised Dietrich's achievements in the film, saying, 'She is a remarkable woman'.

Orson Welles and Dietrich had long discussed working together. Dietrich finally agreed to appear in *Touch of Evil* (1957), in a role written especially for her as the madame of a bordello and long-time mistress of Hank Quinlan (Welles). Dietrich usually only acted for high salaries, but Welles had no money for the production, salaries, or indeed anything else, so she accepted to do the role for nothing. (To be able to use her name to promote the film, Universal eventually paid her a nominal fee of $7,500.)

Dietrich has four scenes and is on screen for about 10 minutes. When Quinlan is shot Dietrich's madame delivers one of her favourite movie lines, 'He was some kind of a man. What does it matter what people say about you?'

Many critics regard this film as the first time that she had matched the performance she gave in *The Blue Angel*. Dietrich and Welles's personal dynamic make them an extraordinary on-screen couple.

In 1961, between the occasional films and her stage work, Doubleday edited the incomplete manuscript of *Beauty is an Illusion* into Dietrich's first book, *Marlene Dietrich's ABC*. It was serialized in *Look Magazine*. The *New York Times* made the comment, 'Viewed over Miss Dietrich's shoulder, the alphabet will never seem the same again.'[137] In this form, Dietrich could give her opinions and a sense of who she was. It has not dated and still makes for wonderful reading.

She recorded regularly and always sent copies of her records to friends. An amusing rumour at the time, was that she had made an hour-long recording, consisting only of her concert ovations. She would then supply a running commentary, 'that is Paris, that is Berlin, that is London . . .'[134]

Judgment at Nuremberg (1961) was Dietrich's last film for a major studio. Set in 1948 at the time of 'de-nazification' and the war crimes tribunals in Germany, it covers the trials not of a major Nazi, but of the German judiciary. The director, Stanley Kramer added Dietrich's part as Mme Bertholt, an aristocratic wife of a German general, as a window into the life of post-war Germany. *Judgment at Nuremberg* is far removed from the triumphalist sentiment and judgemental tone of many post-war films. It features an extraordinary performance by Spencer Tracy as Judge Dan Haywood, a provincial judge, trying to understand how a country and a people could sink into such horror. Dietrich's character embodies the dignity of old Germany, the Prussian morals of her mother's generation.

Spencer helped her through her anxieties about the part,

Spencer Tracy and Dietrich in *Judgment at Nuremberg*, 1961

particularly when she felt her character was distorting the truth. She had enormous difficulties with Mme Bertholt's line 'We did not know!' but without it, Spencer's exit words, 'It came to that the first time you sentenced a man to death you knew to be innocent' would have had no meaning.

Judgment at Nuremberg was a success at the box office, partially due to its star cast. In addition, the film was nominated for eleven Academy Awards, including Best Picture, and won Academy Awards for Maximilian Schell and Abby Mann's script.

After her role in *Judgment at Nuremberg*, Dietrich's next involvement with film, was as narrator for *Black Fox* (1962), an American documentary on Hitler, which won the Academy Award for Best Documentary. Her dignified presentation was much praised by the critics, and her unemotional and matter-of-fact delivery gave the terrible images an even greater impact.

She appeared next in *Paris When it Sizzles* (1963), as a favour to the director, Richard Quine, the cast, William Holden, Audrey Hepburn, and Noël Coward, and as a screen credit to Dior. In her short and essentially pointless cameo, she rushes from her limousine into the House of Dior.

Dietrich's film career was over, and her Las Vegas shows had grown stale. But in 1958, she had the good fortune to hire a young Burt Bacharach to tour with her as her musical director and arranger. What von Sternberg had done for her film image, Bacharach did for her stage appearances, reworking and rearranging her repertoire to fit the limitations of her voice. *[It] was the luckiest break in my professional life,* Dietrich later wrote, *I had dropped into a world about which I knew nothing, and I had suddenly found a teacher. With the force of a volcano erupting, Bacharach reshaped my songs and changed my act into a real show. Later it was to become a first-class 'one-woman's show'.*[148]

Burt Bacharach (1928–) studied cello, drums, and piano and played in several jazz bands in the 1940s. Many of his songs hit the top ten from the mid-1960s on. His most important collaborations were with Marlene Dietrich and Dionne Warwick.

With her new show reshaped by Bacharach, she opened on 31 November 1959 at Théâtre de L'Étoile in Paris, introduced by Maurice Chevalier. Paris loved her, critics and audience alike. It seemed that only Noël Coward, as a friend and fellow performer, noticed that her new style might need further refining.

'[Marlene] has developed a hard, brassy assurance and she belts out every song harshly and without finesse. All her aloof, almost lazy glamour has been overlaid by a noisy, "take-this-and-like-it" method which, to me, is disastrous. However, the public loved it. All the same, I know that they would have loved her even more if she had been more re-mote and not worked so blatantly hard.'[141]

But, writing three years later and after she had toured the show worldwide, he had nothing but admiration for her. '[Marlene] was really marvellous. I have never seen her so good. She has learned a lot during this racketing from capital

Jean Louis's creations metamorphosed me into a perfect, ethereal being, the most seductive there was

Dietrich glittered in sequins and feathers at her Las Vegas performances

to capital, and now puts her numbers over with far more authority and technique.'[142]

Bacharach toured with her for just for two years, but stayed in touch, helping, coaching and encouraging her. Like any man she admired, she lived to please him and trusted him absolutely. He repaid her trust by rarely speaking about her in public.

When Bacharach finally left to pursue his own career in 1965,

Floral tribute in Stockholm, 1963

Dietrich never again changed the shape of her show – although she did work with other musical directors and occasionally added a new song.

During her years on stage, she toured South America, North America, the United Kingdom, Scandinavia, Poland, Holland, Belgium, Switzerland, France, Russia, Australia, South Africa, Spain, and Canada. Her visit to Germany was an important decision for her, as she had not been back since her mother's death. She was greeted with hostile remarks and hate mail, and was even spat at by a young woman. She was picketed with 'Go Home, Marlene' posters; it seemed that some Germans still considered her a traitor to the country.

Halfway through the tour, in Wiesbaden, she missed the edge of the stage and fell into the orchestra pit, breaking her collarbone. She had begun drinking both before and during shows, but if she tumbled from being slightly drunk, the pain sobered her. She never cancelled a performance, simply tied her arm to her side and continued the tour. Despite the controversy from an outspoken minority, it was a huge success. The applause at the performances was intoxicating, so she broke her own rule and gave encores, receiving 18 curtain calls in Berlin and even more in Munich. But the Germany she had left all those years ago had ceased to exist, and soon a wall would divide her native Berlin; she no longer felt she belonged. *The Germans and I do not speak the same language any more,* she told reporters.[143]

Whilst on tour to Israel, she asked the audience if she could sing to them in German. Although the native tongue of many of Israel's inhabitants, the language was still taboo. As she sang 'Lili Marleen' in German the crowd wept.

In 1967, she performed on Broadway, causing major traffic jams as she climbed on to the roof of her limousine to hand out signed photographs. That year she also won a Tony Award for the year's best one-woman show. She accepted the award drunk, embarrassingly stumbling across the platform.

Driven on by her new-found love affair with the audience she worked long hours, never seeming to tire. She was on top of the world and nothing could touch her. But the price of being 'Marlene Dietrich' was high. As her age increased, so did her alcohol intake – she was drinking heavily. For many years her extraordinary self-discipline would help her hide, even suppress, her intoxication when necessary, but towards the end of her public life, she began to lose control.

Dietrich in her extravagant 'Swan Coat' designed to look good when bowing, Queen's Theatre, London

When she came to record her live show for television, in the autumn of 1972, Dietrich had lost her crispness and sex appeal. Her earlier élan was replaced with routine. *I wish you love – an evening with Marlene Dietrich* (1972) is embarrassing and captures very little of what earlier audiences had seen in her live stage performance. Dietrich insisted on recording it outside America, in front of what she felt would be an appreciative audience. Bizzarely, she chose the Soviet Union, and Denmark as venues for her concerts. But she had to settle on filming the show at the New London Theatre, Drury Lane, which was just being completed. Alexander Cohen would direct the show. She was to earn $250,000, with the rights eventually reverting to Maria.

Who knows why they turn out to see me in such numbers. They certainly don't come to see me just because I take all the trouble to look as good as I can . . . But it's because I go out alone that I can be myself, and when they applaud they're applauding maybe what I've done, maybe what I've tried to stand for, or maybe just what they hope I'm going to deliver. Some nights of course they just sit there in stunned silence, amazed that I'm still alive and moving at all.[131]

Dietrich had never liked television and could not understand how it worked. She suffered under the harsh lighting and her sets looked awkward. She also felt abandoned on stage without her conductor Stan Freeman close by. Unlike her paying audience who came to worship her, this studio audience were more interested in the novely of watching themselves being filmed than they were in her performance.

Her close-ups revealed an embittered old lady nostalgic for her youth. She blamed Cohen. By way of response, he sued her for slander, and withheld payment of her fee. She already had other shows lined up and a disappointing television show was bad for her reputation. Even if the vigour of her live shows had paled, she knew she could do better.

Make up – too bad most of us need it.[145]

The Beginning of the End

HEALTH 1965–1980

Dietrich's health had begun to deteriorate as early as 1953. She suffered from unpredictable pains and swellings in her legs. When finally examined, she was found to have arteriosclerosis in both legs, caused by a blockage in the lower arteries. This stopped the normal blood flow in her legs. In addition, she was in the early stages of cervical cancer. Despite these symptoms, she refused to be treated for another decade. She always believed in self-medication, so these new ailments gave her a great opportunity to try the new drugs on the market. She found a couple of glasses of champagne and an injection of vitamin B to be most effective, helping the pain and giving her the sense of restored energy.

By 1965, she was thinner than she had ever been, and still losing weight. Certain that her mother already had an advanced cancer, Maria managed to take her to a doctor. Knowing that Dietrich would never undergo surgery or indeed accept that she was ill, Maria arranged for her to receive radium implants, under the guise of a preventative treatment for possible cancer. Dietrich was terrified of doctors and never comfortable in hospitals; even during the war she had never liked performing in them. They brought back memories of death and decay. Both her father and step-father had died in hospitals; Louis insane as his venereal disease spread, and Eduard among the wounded and dying in a hospital on the Eastern Front.

Dietrich found her legs were still causing her trouble. After each performance, she could barely walk and had to soak her feet in ice to reduce the swelling. There was worse to come. Her doctors were shocked to find that she was still smoking, and insisted she stop immediately, as it would surely worsen her condition.

Smoking was her trademark, a defining feature. Leaning towards a man, cupping his hand in hers as he offered her a light, blowing smoke in his face in seductive disdain – how could Dietrich possibly be Dietrich without that? She quit, but would never accept the danger of smoking.

The famous trousers now became a necessity for hiding Dietrich's still legendary, but swollen, legs. Whether wearing jeans, leather, or cotton outfits, she could easily pretend to be dedicated follower of fashion. For a more feminine look, she hid her misshapen legs and bandages underneath long dresses or in thigh-length boots and short mini-skirts, which of course then became fashionable. Her feet would swell so unpredictably that she was forced to have boots and shoes made in several different sizes, adding an extra trunk to her caravan of thirty-seven valises. And yet, she carried on performing, with no one in the audience aware of her increasing pain. Her drinking worsened along with her unsteadiness. And though she could still stand, she needed the constant support of the curtain or the microphone stand.

On 7 November 1973 at the end of a performance in Maryland, Washington DC, she reached down to the orchestra pit to shake the hand of her conductor, Stan Freeman. Losing her balance she fell in among the musicians. *Stan Freeman [pulled] me down off the stage,* she insisted.[146] Her left leg was ripped open. Carried to her dressing room and examined by doctors, she still refused surgery. The circulation problems in her legs made it impossible for the wound to heal and put her at real

Dietrich in jeans on one of her last visits to her husband's house in 1973

DECEPTION

risk of infection. Naturally, she ignored the doctors and continued her tour. After almost three months the wound had not healed and threatened to turn gangrenous, she finally consented to surgery. Had she waited any longer, she would certainly have lost the leg. On 26 January 1974, she checked into a hospital in Houston and within the next month she received three consecutive vascular surgeries and skin-graft surgeries. By the beginning of April, she was back on a three-month tour, as tenacious as ever.

Soon after returning to her home in Paris on 9 August, she turned awkwardly and fell on her way to bed, breaking her hip. Insisting that French doctors were sure to kill her, she had Maria arrange to fly her to New York for a hip replacement at the Columbia Presbyterian Hospital. Denied alcohol and under hospital-controlled drug intake, she became extremely bellicose, violently rejecting anyone who offered her help.

'My mother lay silent – for the first time since I had known her, utterly helpless – and I had the strangest sensation of feeling suddenly safe, unhurtable. I hadn't realized until that moment how much I still feared her. For one terrible moment . . . Then I turned and left her to the machines that would resurrect her.' MARIA RIVA [147]

The promise of a future engagement made her finally give in to the treatment and recover; she was due to open at the Grosvenor Hotel in London on 11 September 1974, 29 days after her surgery.

Her continuing dependency on alcohol and drugs, even during her performances, began to make her sloppy. She could no longer attract the crowds to fill large theatres and was now hired to entertain in hotels.

Worst of all she felt alone. Josef von Sternberg had died, Ernest Hemingway had shot himself, and amongst the many friends and lovers who had passed away were Erich Maria Remarque, Jean Cocteau, Edith Piaf, Maurice Chevalier, and Noël Coward. Another blow was the death of her sister, Liesel, on 8 March 1975. They had spent a few holidays together, but Dietrich had never reconciled herself to the secrets revealed at the end of the war, veiling their relationship in deceits and half-truths.

In August 1975, Sieber suffered a stroke and was taken to Holy Cross Hospital in San Fernando Valley, before being transferred to UCLA Medical Center in Los Angeles. Maria and Dietrich (on her way to Australia) came to his bedside.

With her husband ill in hospital and unwell herself, Dietrich was beaten, although she would not admit it to herself. Tickets for her shows in Australia had not sold well, and the promoters, hoping to cut their losses, wanted to cancel the tour. But Dietrich was determined to give her audience a last chance to worship her; she would not let them down. One of her trademarks was for floral tributes to be thrown onto the stage at the end of the performance, her audience was encouraged to shower her with roses. Eventually, she had had enough. A Sydney journalist described her 'tottering windup' efforts on stage as 'the bravest, the saddest, [and] most bittersweet . . . [I] had ever seen.'[148]

On 29 September 1975, so drunk that she could hardly stand, she fell at her curtain call. She had broken her thigh bone. Once again Maria arranged for her rescue. She was flown back to the USA in a body cast, initially passing-through UCLA Medical Center, the same hospital that had treated Sieber. On 7 October, she was transferred back to Columbia Presbyterian Hospital. This time her leg would not mend on its own, and was placed in traction. After months of pain and discomfort, she was reluctant to make the effort to try and walk properly. Dietrich never stepped out on stage again.

Sieber had been discharged and was recovering. In the spring of 1976, Dietrich went to visit him. It was to be their last time together. Rudolf Sieber died on 24 June, 1976, aged 79. *I have lost my husband, my most painful loss of all,* she later wrote in her memoirs.[149] Sieber had been her stability, her support and a vital part of her motivation for 50 years. She did not attend his funeral.

Following his death, she was unable to summon the willpower to go back to work again. The following November, Jean Gabin died. Dietrich had lost the last of the men she had loved. Without work, she stayed at home, in the security of her apartment where it mattered less should she fall, and where she could age out of sight.

At the end of her public life, her costly expenses were much reduced, but they had by no means disappeared. She still rented several apartments around the world and introducing economies was difficult for her. With no savings or investments she was broke again by the mid-1970s.

In order to raise much-needed cash, Dietrich accepted a cameo role in the German production, *Just a Gigolo* in 1978, a film featuring David Bowie, set in Berlin. It tells the story of a Prussian war veteran (Bowie) who returns from the dead. He drifts from job to job until he eventually ends up forced to work as a gigolo.

The film brought Kim Novak back to the big screen as well as Dietrich. Maria arranged the deal; her job was to have her mother appear on set 'in condition to perform her contractual duties'.[150] As Dietrich was unwilling to venture to Berlin or indeed out of Paris, the set was rebuilt in a Parisian studio. She arrived for her two days' work, walking with the help of a cane and physically in no shape to film.

Dietrich walked into shot, leaned against a piano (without a cane), sang the title song 'Just a Gigolo' and acted out her lines. The director, David Hemmings later summed up the experience, 'The crew and writer and producer were all there, and when she finished I was supposed to say "Cut!" and I couldn't. The moment was so charged and the spell she cast so total that the beats went by, one-two-three-four, until finally I came to my senses and said "Cut!" and there was – literally – not a dry eye in the house. We had been admitted to a moment of great professional privilege.'[151]

The critics ridiculed what Dietrich had become in comparison to what she had been. For the first time she took her reviews to heart. The film was a mistake; the prostitution of her image for money had gone too far. Showing herself in public had clearly endangered the one thing she truly treasured, her legend. She never let herself be photographed again. When Maximilian Schell, in the documentary

In *Just a Gigolo* (1978). Dietrich lived to regret it her last film. On the photo she wrote *How ugly can you get?*

Marlene (1984) begs to be allowed to film her, she retorts, *I have been photographed to death.*

In 1979, she fell at home once more, receiving a hairline fracture above the hipbone; she finally gave in. Staying in bed was easier. She became a recluse.

THE END OF AN ERA

Sadness. Bitter in childhood, sweet in adolescence, tragic in old age.[152]

Dietrich at Home

RECLUSE 1980–1992

The telephone became Dietrich's primary connection to the world. She spent hours in conversation, and her bills were enormous. As most of her old friends died or withdrew, she rang people whom she had read about and come to admire, and even the occasional fan. She had known some of the best minds of her days and was now reduced to confiding intimate details of her life to such strangers. The accounts that some of them later published stand as a sad testament to her self-imposed isolation, and her pitiful need for companionship and adoration.

She was still in full command of her mental faculties and followed events from her bedside. Having always been an avid reader, though

Dietrich's last telephone and address book. As her old friends began to die, she replaced their numbers with fans, politicians, writers and others she read about and admired. She rarely gave out her number and the bills, which ran into thousands of dollars, are now filed away at the Film Museum in Berlin deprived of literary companions, she devoured books, journals, and newspapers in French, German, and English. She set up her room so that she need never leave it. Everything was within reach: pencils, pens, paper, envelopes, stamps, books, food, liquor, and medication. She had a small fridge for food and a tiny hot plate where she could cook simple meals when she did not order them in. A maid came daily to empty her chamber pot so that she had no need to leave the room.

The longer she was out of the public eye, the more the press yearned for an image of the reclusive star. They never succeeded, despite repeatedly trying to bribe her staff or hiring cranes to allow cameras to peek through her windows. She would only see Maria. Markus Auer, a cook from her favourite German restaurant in Paris, 'Maison d'Allemagne', describes how, the first time he delivered a meal to her room, she spoke with her back to him,

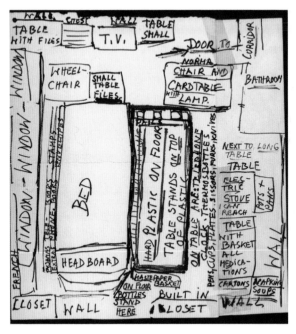

A drawing by Dietrich of her bedroom during the last years of her life

watching his reflection in a mirror. Eventually, as she grew more confident, she would turn to face him and sometimes even greet him in her wheelchair.

In the seclusion of her room, she was able to concentrate on the affirmation of her image. She searched the world for stories and publications concerning herself; at times she would collaborate with writers and journalists, only to denounce them later, when the truths they told were different from the ones she accepted or wished to be publicized. In response to the public demand for more intimate details about her, publishers, writers and the media sought out her family history, picking over her years in Germany, discovering her roles in plays and silent films; writing about her lovers, her problems, her hardships, and her opinions, whether they were true or not. She fought back, litigiously. She often won.

Marlene Dietrich hated biographers. A wonderful example is housed at the Marlene Dietrich Collection. It is a heavily annotated copy of Alexander Walker's *Dietrich* (1984).[153] Nearly every page has a Dietrich-written note in the margin, correcting his facts, accusing him of lying (not always accurately) plastered with comments such as, *all invention; I could kill him; This I can sue on! How un-informed can that man be; He argues with v. Sternberg! The idiot;* or she writes simply: *Rot, Rot. Bullshit, double Bullshit.*

Dietrich had always sought to control her image. Now others, who had never known her, were stealing and profiting from her life. In 'Marlene Dietrich', she had created something beautiful, perfect, and feared the world would destroy it. She should write the definitive biography. Dietrich could not and would not be known as a whore, a bad mother, and a disloyal wife. She might have lived what many saw as an amoral life, but she had tried to be loyal and good to her friends and family. She had once valued her mother's approval above everything else, now her greatest concern was to secure the lasting esteem of Maria and her grandchildren.

Dietrich had been working on her life story for many years. In 1965, she had recruited Hugh Curnow, an Australian journalist, to help her ghost-write her an autobiography for Macmillian Publishers. He was good-looking, 25, and very willing; she brought him back to her apartment in Paris as lover, companion, and adviser, leaving his wife and child behind in Australia. But the collaboration never bore fruit. Curnow returned to his family in Australia, where he tragically died in a freak accident in 1968.

By the beginning of the 1980s her autobiography was still unfinished. Long before, she had been forced to return the advance to Macmillian, only to sign with Simon & Schuster for a further $300,000, whilst supposedly already having a deal with Putnam for $200,000. Simon & Schuster sued her for $3.5 million, and her agent eventually concluded deals with Putnam and Collins in London. Much to her publisher's dismay, and quite contrary to what they believed had been agreed, she refused to write of her many love affairs. She had never given out private information freely, why start now? Facts and dates never meant anything to Dietrich, and she habitually altered events to suit her stories.

Instead, she wrote down what mattered to her, simply how she remembered her life. She wrote about the happiness of her childhood and pride in serving her adopted country during the war, leaving out all of the salacious details. Most of all she wrote expansive tributes to people she had known – and to 'Marlene Dietrich'. The publishers tried to persuade her to produce an extended version, but Dietrich had lost interest and it was shelved. Then, quite suddenly the German publishing house Bertelsmann announced that it was bringing out what it claimed to be her German autobiography, actually translated from the English manuscript. Ten years later this

I am at a loss to protect you and the kids from the frightful image of a mother and grandmother nympho. Maybe you think all this ridiculous. I don't know what you think at the moment because we don't talk. I just wanted you to know that I never had those 'affairs'. . . I want to convince you that I am not as black as they all make me seem. I worshipped my mother, and I would have strangled with my little hands anyone who would have said a word against her . . . I am going to defend my name – and yours come hell or high water. I kiss you, Mass.
MARLENE DIETRICH to Maria, 6 November 1981 [154]

version was finally published in English, translated from a French translation of the German, but it bore little resemblance to Dietrich's original manuscript. As long as she was paid, Dietrich didn't care. If the price was right, she wrote. With her friends and lovers nearly all gone, there was no one left to disagree with her.

At the end of the 1980s, shortly before her death, Maria and she, both in need of money, planned another book. They negotiated the deal with Arnold A Knopf in New York, with a proviso that the book should be published only after Dietrich's death. Having sorted through letters, documents, and her own memories, Maria was ready with her mother's biography soon after she was buried.

MAXIMILIAN SCHELL'S 'MARLENE'

Always glad of an opportunity to make money, Dietrich decided that television might not be such a bad medium, after all. She was looking for a new format to market herself. Encouraged by her narration on *Black Fox*, which helped the documentary to win an Academy Award, she decided to narrate her own documentary. To her mind, it seemed easy, she need not appear on screen but would still be rewarded.

Persuading a production company accept a Dietrich documentary on these terms was difficult, but in 1980 Dietrich started negotiations with OKO Films. Two years passed before her various demands had been met and the contract was signed.

The final documentary would be recorded in both German and English, at her home. She refused to assist, witholding all personal letters, press clippings and archival material. She would be paid an advance of $100,000 for the recording and an extra sum plus a percentage on its sale to television. Oscar winner Maximilian Schell, her fellow actor in *Judgment at Nuremberg*, and now making feature films, was considered the ideal director.

Schell was hesitant to sign at first. He had never made a documentary before and knew that working with Dietrich would not be easy. There was no script and apparently little material from which to create it. Dietrich still refused to appear on camera; the documentary, she insisted, would consist solely of clips from her films, press releases, and perhaps, if it could be found, *The Blue Angel* screen test – this was found in Austria years later.

At the beginning of recording Schell realised that he had nothing usable. Dietrich's drinking was also a problem, and her moods swung constantly between aggression and despair. As Schell had no script, Dietrich agreed to respond to a series of questions. The interviews were a complete failure. Dietrich had never done anything by chance, her strength had always been precision and control. She became angry and resentful that the making of the documentary was not as seamless as she had envisioned.

Clearly drunk from the outset, Dietrich slurs her words. She slips from English into German, hardly lucid in either language. Her answers are either nonsensical or monosyllabic. Schell tried every trick to get her to cooperate, but after days of her intractability, and having taped only five minutes, on the fourth day he walked out.

Schell worked wonders with the little material that he had. The result is an innovatory, fascinating documentary that gives a unique picture of Dietrich both as star and recluse. Schell strips away her professional veneer better than anyone has ever done. She cries at the recollection of her childhood, but is perceptive in her analysis of scenes from von Sternberg's *The Scarlet Empress*. The very lack of Dietrich makes the viewer long for her. The documentary is unfulfilling, but somehow touching and revealing, it is hard to imagine a better critique of the Dietrich legend.

Of course Dietrich disapproved of, even hated the film. Unable to recognize herself in the drunken, angry, woman she was hearing, she was certain her voice had been faked. She demanded that film be re-edited and cut, or preferably destroyed. But when it began to win awards at various international festivals and was nominated for Best Documentary Film at the Academy Awards, she managed to appear pleased with the outcome, at least in public.[155]

Dietrich's breakfast on a morning in November, 1989:
2 freshly baked Bavarian Bagels
4 pieces of pumpernickel
apple and cherry marmalade
150 g of German cold cuts
150g thinly sliced Black Forest ham
a piece of the finest Allgäuer cheese
Black Forest Cherry torte
fruit
Charles Heidsieck Champagne[156]

In June 1984, Dietrich was still waiting for her income from the film. Her bank accounts were empty. Her long-suffering landlord stopped asking for the arrears and issued an eviction notice. The press could not have been more delighted; a movie legend was about to be thrown out on the street; a recluse and an invalid at that. Dietrich was lucky again, Paris had an almost-forgotten law that the bedridden cannot be evicted. She was promoted from Chevalier of the Légion d'Honneur to Commandeur and the city of Paris paid the rent.

The crisis over, Dietrich lay back down in her bed and let the years pass her by. She refused to see old friends; and if someone did come to her door, she pretended to be her own Korean maid. Maria, who was now living in Switzerland again, came to visit often, but never often enough for her mother. Their mind games took on a different form. The mother who had once scrubbed and sterilized her daughter's home now refused to be cleaned and washed, claiming she was being neglected and starved by her own daughter.

'She mixed restorative drinks, and packed parcels and bags filled with lozenges, tablets and onguent as if she was off to the twilight zone. She protected herself against anything from cholera to fish-poisoning, tetanus, circulatory collapse, allergies, toothaches, tinitus, bronchitis, hairloss and seasickness. "You take this in the morning, that at lunch time, that in the evening, this three times a day, this twice, this in an emergency."' HILDEGARD KNEPF, German Actress[157]

She never stopped living to excess. She still ordered exactly what she wanted, and ran up enormous bills. One of her luxuries was a monthly account of more than 6,000 francs with Maison d'Allemagne, until they closed in 1991. They sent her good old-fashioned German food, which pleased her the most. Despite her reclusive existence, she still lived her life as she pleased. In the style of Camille, the once famous, the once beautiful, the once adored 'Marlene Dietrich', now confined to bed, was fading away, neglected and forgotten by the world, which had once worshipped her.

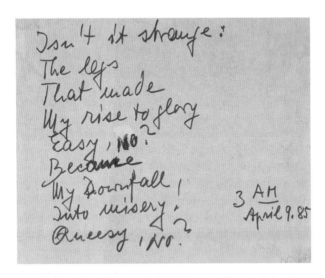

Prolific, fanciful and sad – Dietrich wrote and rewrote her life many times over after she took herself permanently to bed

It is almost impossible to put on paper what one would want done after one is dead.[154]

For Ever After

DEATH 1992

Dietrich had been imagining her own funeral since she first took out life insurance. She had pictured every moment, every grieving face. She had found long ago a perfect spot in the French countryside for her grave, next to a four-star restaurant. Her mourners would be able to eat well after they had paid their tribute.

She imagined that her funeral – organized by Sieber – would be held at l'Église Madeleine, her favourite church in Paris and a suitable complement to her name. She would lie in a simple black dress and Nellie and Dot Pondel would dress her hair and apply her make-up. The bells would ring all over Paris and every friend and lover would attend. Orson Welles would be there, ready to recite *Macbeth* and annoy Noël Coward, who would have prepared a poem. Remarque, forever getting lost, would never make it to the church and Jean Gabin would simply refuse to enter. Sieber could stand at the door handing out red flowers to the ones who had 'made it' [into her bed] and a white flower to the ones who only said they had, as he was the only one who knew the whole truth.

By the time she died, Sieber was long gone. When Dietrich finally passed away on Wednesday 6 May 1992, she had outlived most of her lovers and friends. The Cannes film festival, which had just started, gave her an 'Étoile de Cannes' and dedicated that year's festival to her.

It was Maria who organized her funeral in the Église Madeleine. A simple ceremony was attended by 1,500 people, including her family, friends, and war veterans. As she had wanted and expected, the Parisians crowded around the hearse on the way to the church. A French flag was draped over the casket, in tribute to the city which had been her last home.

Maria then covered the casket with an American flag, as a reminder of her citizenship, and travelled with her mother back to Berlin for the first time since they had left together in 1932. The Wall, which had divided Berlin for nearly 20 years, had fallen three years earlier, uniting the city once more as Dietrich had known it.

It was flower market day, and as the hearse drove through the city hundreds of Berliners threw flowers onto the coffin. She was buried in Schöneberg, under the German flag. Marlene Dietrich had come home at last.

Today, she lies close to her mother's grave, a black marble headstone marking her resting place. Fans come daily with flowers to pay tribute. Flowers were always important in Dietrich's life – she was showered with them by lovers and admirers, her hotel rooms and liner suites had been filled with them. Overshadowed by the memory of her glamorous public image, the real Dietrich of the more ordinary garden flowers, drooping roses, lilacs, violets and tuberoses, is forgotten.

'Hier steh ich an den Marken meiner Tage', translated by Maria Riva as 'Here I stand at the benchmark of my days', which Dietrich interpreted as *I am what I am, I remain the proof of me.*[159]

In the years after her death, books, articles, and documentaries, even a feature film appeared, all trying to recapture the legend of 'Marlene Dietrich'. She still creates headlines, when previously unknown FBI records are released or her (non-existent) connection to Leni Riefenstahl is explored, and her supposed dreams revealed.

In 1993, Maria Riva published her version of Dietrich's life, setting herself up as the definitive authority on her mother's life, revealing much that her mother had kept secret for many years. She angered many of Dietrich's admirers, friends, and fans, who saw her account as vindictive and prejudiced. Maria worked on the book with her mother for a decade and she certainly explores and reveals more than anyone else could have done. In an interview a couple of years after Dietrich's death, Maria explained, 'My mother taught me what to be, by what not to be.' She adds, 'I have great respect for the legend "Marlene Dietrich", the work and dedication it took to create. But I do not respect [my mother] as a human being.'[160]

The centennial of Dietrich's birth in 2002 precipitated more accounts, books and documentaries. Dietrich was posthumously made Honorary Citizen of Berlin in a ceremony attended by her grandson, Peter Riva.

On 24 October 1993, assisted by John Block of Sotheby's in New York, Maria sold the entire Dietrich estate for five million dollars to the City of Berlin and the Stiftung Deutsche Kinemathek.

Dietrich had stored furniture, boxes, and suitcases filled with clothes, books, papers, and artefacts in storage rooms around the world. She moved so frequently, with so little preparation, that she had packed up and forgotten her possessions many times over. During her lifetime, her family had occasionally sold trinkets, letters, cigarette cases, or her last Hollywood car, to pay the storage charges, and support her life in Paris. Maria had always hoped that a museum would buy the entire estate, and agreed to the sale to Berlin despite a larger offer from an individual who planned to make his own

'Marlene Dietrich Shrine'. Either alternative would have amused Dietrich, so long as she was not forgotten. In the long run, a museum seemed the most appropriate facility in which to safeguard her memory. Maria spoke to the press when she arrived with the collection in Berlin. 'Dietrich would have thought the whole fuss ridiculous, but secretly she would have been proud to be brought home.'[161]

Over the next seven years curators restored and sorted through Dietrich's personal belongings. On 26 September 2000, the Film Museum Berlin opened with a permanent exhibit from the Marlene Dietrich Collection. While the museum traces the fascinating history of German film over the last century, Dietrich dominates the exhibition. Her possessions and dresses are restored and displayed, and her beloved mascot dolls, which accompanied her everywhere, sit in a case. The *Blue Angel* screen-test, lost for so many years, is showing on a video-loop, and the beautifully posed, perfectly lit studio portraits, clips from her films, cables, letters, and costumes are on show for all to enjoy. Sorted and coded, the archive holds more than 30,000 pieces of paper and about 20,000 photographs are available for use by researchers from around the world.

With the sale, the family also gave up their own personal letters to Dietrich and handed over ownership to the museum of most of the material, excepting a few 'too personal' objects like Dietrich's childhood diaries, although they too are available for study. Researchers can read the hundreds of love letters and pillow notes sent to Dietrich by her many lovers. Her famous birth certificate, showing her date of birth as 1901, lies in a case next to her American passport, which falsely gives the year as 1904. A lock of golden hair is stuck into an unmarked envelope and lies among love letters from Douglas Fairbanks Jr. One can read Dietrich's most intimate letters, whilst thousands of jotted down memoranda are sorted and packed away. With everything available to read, all Dietrich's secrets are finally exposed.

But would Dietrich have approved of strangers inspecting the minutiae of her life? As she had grown to appreciate Maximilian

Five years after Marlene Dietrich's death her heirs sold the entire contents of her New York apartment at Sotheby's West Coast in Los Angeles. American actress Jennifer Tilly paid more than $11,000 for two letters sent to Marlene Dietrich by the writer Ernest Hemingway and $4,600 for a walking stick given to Dietrich by Noël Coward. The daughter of the late actor Yul Brynner, Victoria Brynner, bought a gold ring her father gave Marlene during their affair. Jean Baptiste Camille Corot's 1874 oil on canvas, *Landscape with Figures and Cows*, was bought by an art dealer for $140,000. An electric alarm clock listed at between $25 and $50 (which Dietrich reportedly used on tours) went for $2,085. A brown Edward Weiss mink coat fetched $1,380 and an *ET* movie poster signed by the director, Steven Spielberg with the words: 'To Marlena, They don't make them like you anymore. From an adoring fan, Steven Spielberg', raised $2,530. (Dietrich's grandson, John Michael Riva worked as art director on Spielberg's *The Color Purple*.) The treasures sold for more than $650,000 to a packed auction room – standing room only available. [162]

Schell's *Marlene*, she might even have grown to like this.

This collection is for the entire world to see, and ensures that she is rediscovered daily. Although never regarded as being as important to the German film industry as her own childhood idol, Henny Porten, or the Danish silent actress, Asta Nielsen, the sheer volume of artefacts and information now available is changing the perception of Dietrich in her native Germany. Dietrich's centrality to this museum, is now set in stone, as her significance as a 20th-century icon overwhelms the reality of her achievements. The images she created are amongst the influential in popular culture.

Facts never mattered to Dietrich. Walking through the museum, surrounded by the objects that represent her life, it is clear that perception and myth had a greater attraction for her, taking the place of a more mundane reality. She sealed herself away behind closed doors for more than a decade to keep her created illusion intact. Her star personality, her teasing eyes are her allure; lovers, and friends gaze at her; this is what most intrigues the film museum's visitors today. For better or for worse, she is remembered, not by the facts of her life, not by her conduct, but as this marvellous creation, existing simply to please an audience – as the legend of 'Marlene

Dietrich'. Whether visitors choose to admire or dislike her is perhaps less relevant to what 'Marlene Dietrich' represents today. Her control of her persona and career was an extraordinary feat which many have tried to repeat, but as a star, an artist, and a woman, she was unique.

> *I am, Gott Sei Dank, a Berliner. I say 'Gott Sei Dank'*
> *as the Berliner humour has always alleviated my spirit*
> *and helped me survive the hardships of life.* [163]

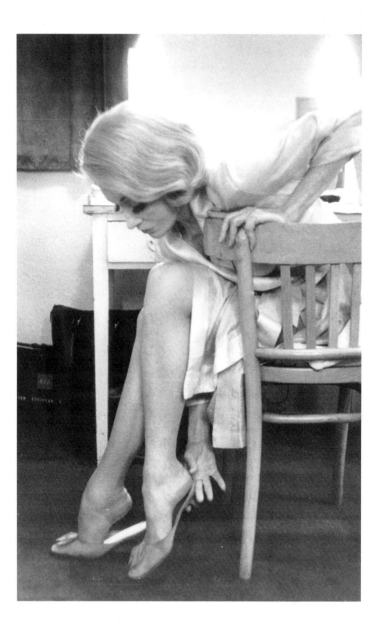

Notes

1 Marlene Dietrich, *Marlene Dietrich's ABC* (1961; reprint, Avon Book Division from New York: Doubleday and Company, 1962), p. 64.

2 Renate Seydel, *Marlene Dietrich: Eine Chronik ihres Lebens in Bildern und Dokumenten* (Henschelverlag, Berlin, 1984), p. 8.

3 Marlene Dietrich, *My Life* (trans: Salvator Attanasio; 1987, Weidenfeld and Nicolson, London, 1989), p. 20.

4 Werner Sudendorf, *Marlene Dietrich* (München: DTV, 2001), p. 15.

5 Steven Bach, *Marlene Dietrich: Life and Legend* (1992, Da Capo Press, London, 2000), p. 19.

6 Maria Riva, *Marlene Dietrich* (Alfred A. Knopf, New York, 1993), p. 785.

7 Dietrich, *My Life*, p. 14; Marlene Dietrich, *Ich bin, Gott sei Dank, Berlinerin* (Ullstein, Müchen, 2000), p. 31.

8 Charles Higham, *Marlene: The life of Marlene Dietrich* (W. W. Norton & Company, New York, 1977), p. 39.

9 Dietrich, *My Life*, p. x.

10 Bach, *Marlene Dietrich: Life and Legend*, p. 20 – quoting from Dietrich's original manuscripts.

11 Higham, *Marlene: The life of Marlene Dietrich*, p. 39.

12 Dietrich, *My Life*, p. 14.

13 Maria Riva, *Marlene Dietrich*, p. 14.

14 Dietrich, *My Life*, p. ix.

15 Dietrich's school notebooks, *Stiftung Deutsche Kinemathe*, Marlene Dietrich Collection, Berlin.

16 Bach, *Marlene Dietrich: Life and Legend*, p. 537.

17 Maria Riva, *Marlene Dietrich*, p. 22.

18 Dietrich, *My life*, p. 20.

19 Bach, *Marlene Dietrich: Life and Legend*, p. 537.

20 Maria Riva, *Marlene Dietrich*, p. 26.

21 Diary: 2 April 1917 in Maria Riva, *Marlene Dietrich*, p. 25.

22 Diary: 14 August 1917 in Maria Riva, *Marlene Dietrich*, p. 29.

23 Dietrich, *My Life*, p. 26; Dietrich, in *Ich bin, Gott sei Dank, Berlinerin – memoiren* 3rd ed., p. 49.

24 'Marlene Dietrich: *"Meine erste Liebe"*,' *Tempo*, Berlin Nr.79, 4th April 1931 – Sudendorf, *Marlene Dietrich*, p. 24.

25 Diary: 7 July 1918 in Maria Riva, *Marlene Dietrich*, p. 32.

26 Diary: 14 August 1917 in Maria Riva, *Marlene Dietrich*, p. 29.

27 Marlene Dietrich, *My Life*, p. 33.

28 Diary: 17 September 1919 in Maria Riva, *Marlene Dietrich*, p. 36.

29 Dietrich, *Marlene Dietrich's ABC*, p. 79.

30 Maria Riva, *Marlene Dietrich*, p. 38.

31 Magdalena Droste , in *Bauhouse-archiv* (reprint, Cologne: Taschen, 1993), p. 22. quoting Bauhaus Manifesto by Walter Gropius 1917, translated by Karen Williams.

32 Bach, *Marlene Dietrich: Life and Legend*, p. 35.

33 Maria Riva, *Marlene Dietrich*, p. 38.

34 Bach, *Marlene Dietrich: Life and Legend*, p. 38.

35 Maria Riva, *Marlene Dietrich*, p. 617.

36 Bach, *Marlene Dietrich: Life and Legend*, p. 42.

37 Dietrich, *Marlene Dietrich's ABC*, p. 21.

38 Dietrich, *My Life*, p. 23.

39 Ibid, p. 32.

40 Maria Riva, *Marlene Dietrich*, p. 37.

41 Bach, *Marlene Dietrich: Life and Legend*, pp. 48–49.

42 Higham, *Marlene: The life of Marlene Dietrich*, p. 47–48.

43 Seydel, *Marlene Dietrich*, p. 84.

44 Dietrich, *My Life*, p. 26.

45 Bach, *Marlene Dietrich: Life and Legend*, p. 43.

46 Seydel, *Marlene Dietrich*, p. 83.

47 Steven Bach, *Marlene Dietrich: Life and Legend*, p. 35. From Dietrich's notes in the marked up version of Alexander Walker, *Dietrich* (New York: Harper & Row, Publishers, 1984), p. 56. – Stiftung Deutsche Kinemathe – Marlene Dietrich Collection Berlin.

48 Dietrich, *Marlene Dietrich's ABC*, p. 149.

49 Seydel, *Marlene Dietrich*, p. 84.

50 Maria Riva, *Marlene Dietrich*, p. 44.

51 Dietrich, *My Life*, pp. 38, 39.

52 Seydel, *Marlene Dietrich*, p. 84.

53 Maria Riva, *Marlene Dietrich*, p. 54.

54 Ibid, p. 43.

55 Higham, *Marlene: The life of Marlene Dietrich*, p. 75; Bach, *Marlene Dietrich: Life and Legend*, p. 69.

56 Bach, *Marlene Dietrich: Life and Legend*, p. 68.

57 Seydel, *Marlene Dietrich*, p. 82.

58 Modris Eksteins, *Rites of Spring*, (1989, London: Bantam Press, 2000), pp. 275–299.

59 Higham, *Marlene: The life of Marlene Dietrich*, p. 71; Seydel, *Marlene Dietrich*, p. 85.

60 Higham, *Marlene: The life of Marlene Dietrich*, p. 65.

61 Dietrich, *My Life*, p. 43.

62 Higham, *Marlene: The life of Marlene Dietrich*, p. 75.

63 Seydel, *Marlene Dietrich*, p. 64.

64 Donald Spoto, *Dietrich* (Bantam, London, 1988), p. 45.

65 Higham, *Marlene: The life of Marlene Dietrich*, p. 77.

66 Dietrich, *Marlene Dietrich's ABC*, p. 129.

67 Josef von Sternberg, *The Blue Angel*, (Lorrimer Publishing, London 1968), p. 9.

68 Leni Riefenstahl, *The Sieve of Time: The Memoirs of Leni Riefenstahl* (Quartet Books Ltd, 1992), p. 77.

69 Stiftung Deutsche Kinemathe-Marlene Dietrich Collection Berlin. – *Newsletter* 42, 16 August, 2002.

70 Bach, *Marlene Dietrich: Life and Legend*, p. 10.

71 Maria Riva, *Marlene Dietrich*, p. 61.

72 von Sternberg, *The Blue Angel*, p. 12.

73 Documentary: '*Das Zweite Leben der Marlene*', dir. Christian and Matt Bauer, 1994.

74 Maria Riva, *Marlene Dietrich*, p. 76.

75 Marlene Dietrich, *Marlene Dietrich's ABC*, p. 134.

76 Quoting *Börsenkurier*, 2 April: Donald Spoto, *Dietrich*, p. 58.

77 Donald Spoto, *Dietrich*, p. 58.

78 Letter, New York City, 10 April 1950 in Maria Riva, *Marlene Dietrich*, p. 83.

79 Bach, *Marlene Dietrich: Life and Legend*, p. 127.

80 Josef von Sternberg, *Fun in a Chinese Laundry* (New York: The Macmillian Company, 1965), p. 246.

81 Maria Riva, *Marlene Dietrich*, p. 84.

82 Sheridan Morley, *Marlene Dietrich* (1976; reprint, Great Britain: Sphere Books limited, 1978), p. 34.

83 W. K. Marin, *Marlene Dietrich – lives of notable gay men and lesbians*, (Chelsea House Publishers, New York, 1994), p. 62; Morley, *Marlene Dietrich*, p. 36.

84 Maria Riva, *Marlene Dietrich*, pp. 90–91.

85 Ibid, p. 92.

86 Dietrich, *My Life*, pp. 55–56.

87 Bach, *Marlene Dietrich: Life and Legend*, p. 137.

88 Maria Riva, *Marlene Dietrich*, p. 110; Bach, *Marlene Dietrich: Life and Legend*, p. 148.

89 Maria Riva, *Marlene Dietrich*, p. 123.

90 Ibid, p. 165.

91 von Sternberg, *Fun in a Chinese Laundry*, p. 264.

92 Nancy Nelson, *Evenings with Cary Grant*, (William Morrow & Co., New York, 1991), p. 69.

93 Maria Riva, *Marlene Dietrich*, p. 110.

94 Ibid, p. 134.

95 von Sternberg, *Fun in a Chinese Laundry*, p. 269.

96 Maria Riva, *Marlene Dietrich*, p. 178.

97 Bach, *Marlene Dietrich: Life and Legend*, p. 418.

98 Morley, *Marlene Dietrich*, p. 51.

99 Dietrich, *My Life*, p. 192.

100 Maria Riva, *Marlene Dietrich*, p. 178.

101 Ibid, p. 343.

102 *The New York Times*, 7 October 1937, (Quoting *Der Stürmer*, March 6 1937)

103 Dietrich, *Marlene Dietrich's ABC*, p. 7.

104 Maria Riva, *Marlene Dietrich*, p. 348.

105 von Sternberg, *Fun in a Chinese Laundry*, p. 253.

106 Homer Dickens, *The Films of Marlene Dietrich* (1968; reprint, Secaucus, New Jersey: The Citadel Press, 1980), p. 131.

107 Higham, *Marlene: The life of Marlene Dietrich*, p. 176.

108 Maria Riva, *Marlene Dietrich*, pp. 169–70.

109 Douglas Fairbanks, jr., *The Salad Days* (reprint, Collins: London, 1988), p. 260.

110 Ibid, p. 261.

111 Maria Riva, *Marlene Dietrich*, p. 428.

112 Higham, *Marlene: The life of Marlene Dietrich*, p. 180.

113 Riva, *Marlene Dietrich*, p. 439.

114 Dietrich, *Marlene Dietrich's ABC*, p. 84.

115 Dietrich, *My Life*, p. 161.

116 Letter to Rudi from Dietrich, Paris 5 December, 1945 – Stiftung Deutsche Kinemathe-Marlene Dietrich Collection Berlin.

117 *Ladies Home Journal*, October 1951 p. 54; Donald Spoto, *Dietrich*, p. 144.

118 On cassette cover of Ray Enricht's 'The Spoilers' – May 1942 Charles K. Feldman Group for Universal Pictures.

119 Dietrich, *Marlene Dietrich's ABC*, p. 152.

120 Ibid, p. 151.

121 Dietrich, *My Life*, p. 60.

122 Ibid, p. 185.

123 Maria Riva, *Marlene Dietrich*, p. 541.

124 Marlene's English Version Lyrics: Hans Leip; Music: Norbert Schultze, English Words: Tommie Conner

125 Maurice Chevalier, *With Love*, (Cassell, London. 1960) *p. 276*.

126 Documentary, David Riva's *Marlene Dietrich, Her Own Song*, 2002.

127 Letter from Dietrich to Maria, Thanksgiving 1945 – Stiftung Deutsche Kinemathe–Marlene Dietrich Collection Berlin.

128 Dietrich, *Marlene Dietrich's ABC*, p. 35.

129 Marlene Dietrich, *My Life*, p. 120.

130 Georg A. Weth, *Ich will wat Feinet: Das Marlene Dietrich Kochbuch*, (Rüten & Loening, Berlin, 2001), p. 15.

131 Maria Riva, *Marlene Dietrich*, pp. 600, 607.

132 Dietrich, *Marlene Dietrich's ABC*, p. 133.

133 Dietrich, *My Life*, p. 203.

134 Ibid, p. 216.

135 Noël Coward tribute to Dietrich, 20 June 1954, Live at Café de Paris, London.

136 Letter from Dietrich to Maria, 13 July, 1958 – Stiftung Deutsche Kinemathe–Marlene Dietrich Collection Berlin.

137 Dickens, *The Films of Marlene Dietrich*, p. 30.

138 Higham, *Marlene: The life of Marlene Dietrich*, p. 288. The record is in the Stiftung Deutsche Kinemathe – Marlene Dietrich Collection Berlin.

139 Marlene Dietrich, *My Life*, p. 157.

140 Dietrich, *My Life*, p. 206.

141 Graham Payn and Sheridan Morley, ed, *The Nöel Coward Diaries*, (Weidenfeld and Nicolson, London, 1982), p. 422.

142 Ibid, p. 505.

143 *Variety* article; Donald Spoto, *Dietrich*, p. 249.

144 Dietrich to author; Sheridan Morley, *Marlene Dietrich*, p. 73.

145 Dietrich, *Marlene Dietrich's ABC*, p. 88.

146 Maria Riva, *Marlene Dietrich*, p. 728.

147 Ibid, p. 736.

148 Mike Gibson 24 September 1975 (*Daily Telegraph* Sydney, Australia) in Maria Riva, *Marlene Dietrich*, p. 752 and *The Sun* (Sydney, Australia), 30 September 1975 in Donald Spoto, *Dietrich*, p. 262.

149 Dietrich, *My Life*, p. 229.

150 Maria Riva, *Marlene Dietrich*, p. 760.

151 Bach, *Marlene Dietrich: Life and Legend*, p. 450.

152 Dietrich, *Marlene Dietrich's ABC*, p. 125.

153 Alexander Walker, *Dietrich* (reprint, New York: Harper & Row, Publishers, 1984),pp. 20, 32, 58, 66 – Stiftung Deutsche Kinemathe – Marlene Dietrich Collection Berlin.

154 Letter from Dietrich to Maria, 6 November 1981 – Stiftung Deutsche Kinemathe – Marlene Dietrich Collection Berlin.

155 Documents, letters and contracts related to the film *Marlene* – Stiftung Deutsche Kinemathe – Marlene Dietrich Collection Berlin.

156 George A. Weth, *Ich will wat Feinet: Das Marlene Dietrich Kochbuch*, (Rütten & Loening, Berlin 2001), pp. 13–14.

157 Ibid, p. 86.

158 Dietrich, *Marlene Dietrich's ABC*, p. 158.

159 Stiftung Deutsche Kinemathe – Marlene Dietrich Collection Berlin – (*Newsletter No. 42 August 16*, 2002), p. 3.

160 Christian and Matt Bauer's Documentary, *Das Zweite Leben der Marlene*, 1994.

161 Christian and Matt Bauer's Documentary, *Das Zweite Leben der Marlene*, 1994.

162 *BBC News*, Sunday, November 2, 1997

163 MSS translation, Marlene Dietrich, in *Ich bin, Gott sei Dank, Berlinerin – memoiren* 3rd ed., p.5

Chronology

History	Culture
1901 Queen Victoria dies; Edward VII becomes king. US President William McKinley assassinated; Theodore Roosevelt becomes president. Boxer Rebellion ends.	Sigmund Freud, *The Psychopathology of Everyday Life*. Anton Chekhov, *The Three Sisters*. Pablo Picasso begins Blue Period.
1907 Anglo-Russian entente. Electric washing machine invented	Joseph Conrad, *The Secret Agent*. Rainer Maria Rilke, *Neue Gedichte*
1908 Bulgaria becomes independent. Austria-Hungary annexes Bosnia-Herzegovina.	Gustav Mahler, *Das Lied von der Erde* (until 1909). Cubism begins with Picasso and Braque.
1912 Balkan Wars (until 1913). ANC formed in South Africa. *Titanic* sinks. Morocco becomes French protectorate. Dr Sun Yat-sen establishes Republic of China.	Arnold Schoenberg, *Pierrot lunaire*. Carl Jung, *The Psychology of the Unconscious*. Bertrand Russell, *The Problems of Philosophy*.
1914 28 June: Archduke Franz Ferdinand assassinated in Sarajevo. First World War begins. Panama Canal opens. Egypt becomes British protectorate.	James Joyce, *The Dubliners*. Ezra Pound, *Des Imagistes*.
1916 Battle of Somme. Battle of Jutland. Easter Rising in Ireland. Arabs revolt against Ottoman Turks.	Guillaume Apollinaire, *Le poète assassiné*. G B Shaw, *Pygmalion*. Dada movement launched.
1919 Treaty of Versailles. Spartacist revolt in Germany. Poland, Hungary, Czechoslovakia, Estonia, Lithuania, and Latvia become republics. Comintern held in Moscow. Prohibition in US. Irish Civil War (until 1921).	Kafka, *In the Penal Colony*. J M Keynes, *The Economic Consequences of the Peace*. The Bauhaus founded in Weimar. United Artists formed.
1921 National Economic Policy in Soviet Union.	Sergei Prokofiev, *The Love of Three Oranges*. Aldous Huxley, *Crome yellow*. Chaplin, *The Kid*.
1922 Soviet Union formed. Benito Mussolini's fascists march on Rome.	T S Eliot, *The Waste Land*. Joyce, *Ulysses*.
1923 Ottoman empire ends. Palestine, Trans-jordan and Iraq to Britain; Syria to France.	Le Corbusier, *Vers une architecture*.
1924 Vladimir Lenin dies.	E M Forster, *A Passage to India*. Kafka, *The Hunger Artist*.
1927 Joseph Stalin comes to power. Charles Lindbergh flies across Atlantic.	Martin Heidegger, *Being and Time*. BBC public radio launched.

1928	Makes first record with songs from her notorious appearance in the revue *Es liegt in der Luft* (*It's in the air*).
1929	First German lead (with Fritz Kortner) in *Die Frau, nach man sich sehnt*, directed by Kurt Bernhardt. October, auditions, is screen tested and contracted for *The Blue Angel* directed by Josef von Sternberg
1930	February, signs with Paramount Pictures through their Berlin office. 1 April, the première of *The Blue Angel* in the Gloria-Palast in Berlin. Departs for the United States that night, leaving behind her daughter and husband. November 14, her first American film, *Morocco* is premièred. Is nominated for a Best Actress Academy Award.
1930–1	6 December–16 April, Last visit to Berlin until 1945. Brings her daughter out to live in Beverly Hills. Her husband moves to Paris with his mistress Tamara Matul (Tami) to work for Paramount.
1931	Stars in *Dishonored*.
1932	Is sued by Josef von Sternberg's ex-wife in a alienation-of-affections case; collaborates with von Sternberg on *Shanghai Express*, writes and performs in *Blonde Venus*.
1933	Begins affair with Mercedes de Acosta; appears in *Song of Songs*, her first film not directed by von Sternberg; rejects offer from Nazi officials to make movies in Germany. Visits Europe but not Germany.
1934	Stars as Catherine the Great in Josef von Sternberg's *The Scarlet Empress*.
1935	Makes her last film with Josef von Sternberg; after seven films together they part ways.
1936	Reveals a flair for comedy in Frank Borzage's *Desire*; appears in her first Technicolor film, *The Garden of Allah*.
1937	Becomes the highest-paid female film star from her salary for the British film, *Knight Without Armour*, 6 March, becomes an American citizen and denounces the German government; stars in box-office disappointment *Angel*; is released from her Paramount contract.
1939	Reinvents herself in the western *Destry Rides Again* starring James Stewart.

History	Culture
1928 Kellogg-Briand Pact for Peace. Alexander Fleming discovers penicillin.	Maurice Ravel, *Boléro*. Kurt Weill, *The Threepenny Opera*.
1929 Lateran Treaty. Yugoslav kingdom under kings of Serbia. Wall Street crash. Young Plan for Germany.	Virginia Woolf *A Room of One's Own*; Noël Coward, *Bitter Sweet*.
1930 London Round-Table Conferences on India. Mahatma Gandhi leads Salt March in India. Frank Whittle patents turbo-jet engine. Pluto discovered.	W H Auden, *Poems*. T S Eliot, 'Ash Wednesday'. William Faulkner, *As I lay Dying*. Evelyn Waugh, *Vile Bodies*.
1931 King Alfonso XIII flees; Spanish republic formed. Ramsay MacDonald leads national coalition government in Britain. New Zealand becomes independent. Japan occupies Manchuria. Building of Empire State Building completed.	
1932 Kingdom of Saudi Arabia independent. Kingdom of Iraq independent. James Chadwick discovers neutron. First auto-bahn opened between Cologne and Bonn.	Aldous Huxley, *Brave New World*.
1933 Nazi Party wins German elections. Adolf Hitler appointed chancellor. Hitler forms Third Reich. F D Roosevelt president in US; launches New Deal.	André Malraux, *La condition humaine*. Gertrude Stein, *The Autobiography of Alice B Toklas*.
1934 Night of the Long Knives in Germany. Long March in China. Enrico Fermi sets off controlled nuclear reaction.	Dmitri Shostakovich, *The Lady Macbeth of Mtsensk*. Henry Miller, *Tropic of Cancer*.
1935 Nuremberg Laws in Germany. Philippines becomes self-governing. Italy invades Ethiopia.	George Gershwin, *Porgy and Bess*. R Strauss, *Die Schweigsam Frau*. Marx Bros, *A Night at the Opera*.
1936 Rhineland occupied by Germany. Edward VIII abdicates throne. George VI becomes king. Léon Blum forms 'Popular Front' government in France. Anti-Comintern Pact between Japan and Germany. Spanish Civil War (until 1939).	Prokofiev, *Peter and the Wolf*. A J Ayer, *Language, Truth and Logic*. BBC public television founded.
1937 Arab-Jewish conflict in Palestine. Japan invades China. Nanjing massacre. Photocopier patented in US.	Jean-Paul Sartre, *La Nausée*. John Steinbeck, *Of Mice and Men*. Picasso, *Guernica*.
1939 Stalin and Hitler sign non-aggression pact. 1 September: Germany invades Poland. Russo-Finnish war begins. Francisco Franco becomes dictator of Spain. Britain and France declare war on Germany. Faisal II becomes king of Iraq.	Steinbeck, *The Grapes of Wrath*. John Ford, *Stagecoach* with John Wayne. David O Selznick, *Gone with the Wind* with Vivien Leigh and Clark Gable.

Year	Life
1940	*Stars in Seven Sinners.*

1944–5 Entertains American troops in North Africa and Europe; she makes a series of propaganda broadcasts from London called 'Marlene sings to her homeland'.

1945 September, Dietrich her mother in Berlin for the first time since the beginning of the war. Also meets with her sister, Liesel in Bergen-Belsen. 3 November, her mother dies and is buried in Berlin. Dietrich repatriated to the United States at the end of the war.

1947 4 July, Dietrich's daughter, Maria marries William Riva in the St John The Divine Episcopal Cathedral in New York. (Dietrich is not present.) 18 November, Major Gen. Maxwell D Taylor awards her US Medal of Freedom for her action in the war, the highest honour for a civilian.

1948 28 June, Dietrich's first grandchild, John Michael Riva is born. Is proclaimed 'The world's most glamorous Grandmother'. Acts the part of Erika von Schlütow in Wilder's *Foreign Affair.*

1950 Is awarded the title of 'Chevalier de la Legion d'Honneur' by the French government (in 1971 she was promoted 'Officier' by President Pompidou and in 1989 to 'Commandeur' by President Mitterand). Alfred Hitchcock casts her in *Stage Fright.*

1951 Plays the part of Monica Teasdale in *No Highway in the Sky.*
1952 Appears in Fritz Lang's *Rancho Notorious.*

1953 Is Master of Ceremonies in the gala charity event at Madison Square Garden.

1953–4 Performes at the Hotel Sahara in Las Vegas and Café de Paris in London. Launches a career in cabaret.

History	Culture
1940 Germany occupies France, Belgium, the Netherlands, Norway and Denmark. Vichy government in France. Britain retreats from Dunkirk. Winston Churchill becomes PM in Britain. Battle of Britain begins. Leon Trotsky assassinated.	Graham Greene, *The Power and the Glory*. Ernest Hemingway, *For Whom the Bell Tolls*. Chaplin, *The Great Dictator*. Disney, *Fantasia*.
1944 Normandy invasion. Paris is liberated. Arnhem disaster. Civil war in Greece.	Jorge Luis Borges, *Fictions*. Sergei Eisenstein, *Ivan the Terrible*. Laurence Olivier, *Henry V*.
1945 Yalta Agreement. 8 May: Germany surrenders. UN formed. Clement Attlee becomes PM in Britain. Postdam conference. Roosevelt dies; Truman becomes US president. Atomic bombs dropped on Hiroshima and Nagasaki. Burma road to China re-opened. 2 September: Japan surrenders. Wars of independence begin in Indo-China and Indonesia. Civil war in China.	Benjamin Britten, *Peter Grimes*. George Orwell, *Animal Farm*. Karl Popper, *The Open Society and Its Enemies*. UNESCO founded.
1947 Puppet Communist states in Eastern Europe. India becomes independent. Chuck Yeager breaks the sounds barrier.	Tennessee Williams, *A Streetcar named Desire*. Albert Camus, *The Plague*. Anne Frank, *The Diary of Anne Frank*. Jean Genet, *The Maids*.
1948 Marshall Plan (until 1951); Berlin airlift. Welfare state created in Britain. Malayan emergency begins (until 1960). Apartheid legislation in South Africa. Gandhi is assassinated.	Bertolt Brecht, *The Caucasian Chalk Circle*. Greene, *The Heart of the Matter*. Norman Mailer, *The Naked and the Dead*. Alan Paton, *Cry, the Beloved Country*.
1950 Schuman Plan. Korean War begins. China conquers Tibet. Stereophonic sound invented. First successful kidney transplant.	Pablo Neruda, *Canto General*. Eugène Ionesco, *The Bald Prima Donna*. Billy Wilder, *Sunset Boulevard*.
1951 Anzus pact in Pacific.	J D Salinger, *The Catcher in the Rye*.
1952 Gamal Abdel Nasser leads coup in Egypt. European Coal and Steel Community formed; Britain refuses to join. Elisabeth II becomes queen of Britain. McCarthy era begins in US.	Hemingway, *The Old Man and the Sea*. Samuel Beckett, *Waiting for Godot*. *High Noon* with Gary Cooper and Grace Kelly.
1953 Stalin dies. Egyptian Republic formed. Mau Mau rebellion in Kenya (until 1957). Dwight Eisenhower inaugurated US president. Korean war ends. Francis Crick and James Watson discover double helix structure of DNA. Colour TV begins in US.	William Burroughs, *Junkie*. Dylan Thomas, *Under Milk Wood*. Arthur Miller, *The Crucible*. Federico Fellini, *I Vitelloni*.

1955	Appears in Las Vegas with Noël Coward. Hires the young Burt Bacharach as her arranger, conductor, and accompanist. They work together for ten years.
1956	Has a cameo in *Around the World in 80 Days*.
1957	Stars in a double role in Billy Wilder's *Witness for the Prosecution*.
1958	As a favour to her friend, Orson Welles, gives a cameo performance as a gypsy fortune-teller in his *Touch of Evil*.
1960	First German tour.
1961	Appears in *Judgment at Nuremberg*.
1962	Narrates *Black Fox*, the anti-Hitler documentary.
1963	Writes her first book, *Dietrich's ABC*.
1964	Makes a guest appearance in *Paris when it Sizzles*. Russian tour with cancellations in Moscow and Leningrad.
1965	March, receives radium implant treatment for cervical cancer. Tami dies in a hospital for the mentally ill. Dietrich opens in Johannesburg 3 $^1/_2$ weeks after treatment.
1967	Opens in her debut on Broadway with a one-woman show at Lunt-Fontanne Theatre, New York City. The street clogs with nightly traffic jams.

History	Culture
1955 West Germany joins NATO. Warsaw Pact formed.	James Baldwin, *Notes of a Native Son*. Vladimir Nabokov, *Lolita*. Satyajit Ray, *Pather Panchali*.
1956 Twentieth Congress of Soviet Party; Nikita Khruschev denounces Stalin. Suez Crisis. Revolts in Poland and Hungary. Fidel Castro and 'Che' Guevara land in Cuba. Morocco becomes independent. Civil war in Vietnam.	Elvis Presley, 'Heartbreak Hotel', 'Love Me Tender'. John Osborne, *Look Back in Anger*.
1957 Treaty of Rome; EEC formed. Sputnik 1 launched. Ghana becomes independent.	Bernstein/Sondheim *West Side Story*. Jack Kerouac, *On the Road*.
1958 Fifth French Republic; Charles De Gaulle becomes president of France. Pope John XXIII elected. Great Leap Forward launched in China (until 1960). Castro leads revolution in Cuba. Texas Instruments invents silicon chip.	Chinua Achebe, *Things fall Apart*. Boris Pasternak, *Dr Zhivago*. J K Galbraith, *The Affluent Society*. Claude Lévi-Strauss, *Structural Anthropology*. Harold Pinter, *The Birthday Party*.
1960 U2 affair. Sharpeville Massacre in South Africa. Congo becomes independent. Cyprus becomes independent. Vietnam war begins (until 1975). OPEC formed. Nigeria becomes independent. Oral contraceptives marketed.	Fellini, *La Dolce Vita*. Alfred Hitchcock, *Psycho*.
1961 Berlin Wall erected. Bay of Pigs invasion. Yuri Gagarin first man in space.	Rudolf Nureyev defects. François Truffaut, *Jules et Jim*.
1962 Cuban missile crisis. Second Vatican Council (until 1965). Jamaica, Trinidad and Tobago, and Uganda become independent. Satellite television launched.	Alexander Solzhenitsyn, *One Day in the Life of Ivan Denisovich*. David Lean, *Lawrence of Arabia*.
1963 J F Kennedy assassinated; Johnson president of US. Martin Luther King leads March on Washington. French veto Britain's bid to join the EEC. Nuclear Test-ban Treaty. Kenya becomes independent. Organisation of African Unity formed.	The Beatles, 'She Loves You' and 'I want to hold your hand'. *Cleopatra* with Richard Burton and Elizabeth Taylor. Luchino Visconti, *The Leopard*.
1964 Khruschev ousted by Leonid Brezhnev. First race relations act in Britain. Civil Rights Act in US. PLO formed. Word processor invented.	Saul Bellow, *Herzog*. Stanley Philip Larkin, *The Whitsun Weddings*. Kubrick, *Doctor Strangelove*.
1965 Military coup in Indonesia. Indo-Pakistan war.	The Beach Boys, 'California Girls'. Joe Orton, *Loot*. Harold Pinter, *The Homecoming*.
1967 Six day war. Martin Luther King assassinated.	The Beatles, *Sergeant Pepper's Lonely Hearts Club Band*. Kubrick, *2001: A Space Odyssey*.

Year	Life
1972	1 January, Maurice Chevalier dies. Dietrich airs her first television special, shot in London, *I wish you love*.
1973	26 March, Noël Coward dies. 8 May sister, Liesel dies. 18 November concert in Washington, falls off the stage into the orchestra pit and hurts her leg. Continues tour despite the wound.
1974	26 January, given a skin and bypass operation by Dr Michael de Bakey in Houston, Texas. 10 August, falls in her Paris apartment and breaks her left hip; 13 August Dr Frank E Stinchfield operates on her at the Columbia Presbyterian Hospital, New York.
1975	Last tour (Belgium, Netherlands, Britain, Canada, US and Australia). 29 September, in Sydney, slips and falls. breaks her left thigh bone and is transported to Dr Frank Stinchfield in New York. Bedridden, she takes four months to heal.
1976	April–May, visits her husband, Rudi, for the last time at his farm in California. 24 June, Rudolf Sieber dies. Dietrich is not present at his funeral. 15 November, Jean Gabin dies. 4 December, Dietrich's first great-grandchild, John Matthew Riva is born in London.
1978	Last film performance in *Just a Gigolo*.
1979	Autobiography is published in German as *Nehmt Nur mein Leben*. It is later translated into French and English as *Marlene Dietrich, My life*. Suffers another fall causing a hairline fracture about the hip joint, cured by four weeks' bedrest. Decides to stay in bed.
1982–3	Maximilian Schell makes his award-winning documentary *Marlene*, a biographical film on Dietrich – only her voice appears.
1992	6 May, Dietrich dies in her sleep in Paris; 14 May, 1,500 people attend her funeral in the Madeleine Church in Paris; 16 May, she is buried in Berlin in the same cemetery as her mother.
1993	24 October, Dietrich's daughter, Maria Riva presents the Dietrich estate to the State of Berlin and the Stiftung Deutsche Kinemathek, assisted by John Block of Sotheby's (New York).
2000	26 September, the Film Museum in Berlin opens with a permanent exhibition from the Marlene Dietrich Collection.

History	Culture
1972 US/Soviet Union detente. SALT 1 signed. US recognizes Communist China. Uganda expels Asians. Bloody Sunday massacre (N Ireland). Salvador Allende overthrown in Chile; Augusto Pinchet takes power. World Trade Center completed. Optical fibre is invented.	Luciano Berio, *Concerto for Two Pianos*. Richard Adams, *Watership Down*. Bertolucci, *Last Tango in Paris*. Francis Ford Coppola, *The Godfather*.
1973 Yom Kippur war. Denmark, Ireland, and Britain enter EEC. US withdraws from Vietnam war. OPEC oil crisis.	Pink Floyd, *The Dark Side of the Moon*. Larkin, *High Windows*. François Truffaut, *Day for Night*. Solzhenitsyn is expelled from the Soviet Union.
1974 Watergate scandal; US President Richard Nixon forced to resign. Cyprus invaded by Turkey. Haile Selassie deposed in Ethiopia. Three-day week in Britain.	
1975 Franco dies; King Juan Carlos restored in Spain. Angola and Mozambique become independent. End of Vietnamese war. Khmer Rouge seize power in Cambodia. Civil War in Lebanon. Helsinki Accords. Apollo and Soyuz dock in space.	Pierre Boulez, *Rituel in memoriam Bruno Maderna*. Queen, 'Bohemian Rhapsody'; first major rock video. Dario Fo, *Can't Pay? Won't Pay!* Steven Spielberg, *Jaws*.
1976 Chairman Mao Zedong dies. Soweto massacre.	Alex Haley, *Roots*.
1978 Pope John Paul II elected. Camp David Accord. Boat people begin to leave Vietnam. Civil wars in Chad and Nicaragua. First test-tube baby born.	John Irving, *The World According to Garp*. Iris Murdoch, *The Sea The Sea*. Michael Cimino, *The Deer Hunter*. First broadcast of *Dallas*.
1979 'Winter of discontent' strikes in Britain. Margaret Thatcher becomes prime minister. Iranian revolution; Iran hostage crisis. Soviet Union invades Afghanistan. Pol Pot deposed in Cambodia.	Milan Kundera, *The Book of Laughter and Forgetting*. V S Naipaul, *A Bend in the River*. Woody Allen, *Manhattan*. Terry Jones, *Monty Python's Life of Brian*.
1982 Falkland Islands conflict. Israel invades Lebanon. Famine in Ethiopia. Compact discs introduced commercially.	Michael Jackson, *Thriller*. Richard Attenborough, *Gandhi*. Spielberg, *ET*.
1992 Bosnian war. Britain withdraws from Exchange Rate Mechanism. Famine in eastern and southern Africa.	Michael Ondaatje, *The English Patient*. Tony Kushner, *Angels in America*.

List of Works

Der Grosse Bariton/The Great Bariton by Leo Ditrichstein and Fred and Fanny Hutton, dir: Eugen Robert [a fan], Berlin, 20 January 1922.

Pandora's Box/Die Büchse der Pandora by Frank Wedekind, dir: Carl Heine [Ludmilla Steinherz] Berlin, 7 September 1922.

The Taming of the Shrew by William Shakespeare, dir: Iwan Schmith (after Max Reinhardt) [the Widow] Berlin, 2 October 1922.

Timotheus in flagranti by Charles-Maurice Hannequin and Pierre Véber, dir: Iwan Smith [Suzanne, Anne-Marie, and Miss Simpson] Berlin, 11 January 1923.

The Circle/Der Kreis by W Somerset Maugham, dir: Bernhardt Reich [Anna Shenstone] Berlin, 24 January 1923.

Penthesilea by Heinrich von Kleist, dir: Richard Révy [an Amazon] Berlin, 6 February 1923.

Between Nine and Nine/Zwischen Neun under Neun by Hans Sturm [alternating daughter and mother] Berlin, Summer 1923.

My Cousin Eduard/Mein Vetter Eduard by Fred Robs, dir: Ralph Athur Roberts [Lilian Berley] Berlin, 12 September 1923.

A Midsummer Night's Dream by William Shakespeare, dir: Reinhard Bruck [Hippolyta] Berlin, 9 February 1924.

Frülings Erwachen/Spring Awakening, dir: Frank Wedeland [Ilse] Berlin, 23 February 1924.

When the Young Vine Blossoms/Wenn der neue Wein wieder Blüht by Bjornstern Bjornson, dir: Reinhard Bruck [unknown role] Berlin, 8 March 1924.

The Imaginary Invalid/Der Einbildete Kranke by Molière, [Toinette, a servant girl] Berlin, April 1924.

Back to Methuselah by George Bernard Shaw, dir: Victor Barnowsky [Eve] Berlin, 26 November 1925.

Back to Methuselah by George Bernard Shaw, dir: Victor Barnowsky [Eve] Berlin, 24 January 1926.

Duel on the Lido/Duell am Lido by Hans Rehfisch, dir: Victor Martin Kerb [Lou Carrere, the daughter] Berlin, 20 February 1926.

The Rubicon/Der Rubicon by Eugène Bourdet, dir: Ralph Arthur Roberts [unknown role] Berlin, 4 April 1926.

From Mouth to Mouth/Von Mund zu Mund by Hans J. Rehfisch, dir: Leopold Jessner [Mistress of Ceremonies] Berlin, 20 February 1926.

Three's Company/Wenn man zu dritt by/dir: Max Brod [unknown role] Vienna, summer 1927.

Broadway by George Abbot and Philip Dunning, dir: Franz Wenzler [Rubie] Vienna 20 September 1927.

Die Schule von Uznach oder Neue Sachlichkeit by Carl Sternheim, dir: Emil Geyer, Vienna, 28 November 1927.

Broadway by George Abbott and Philip Dunning, dir: Eugen Robert [Rubie] Berlin, 9 March 1928.

Nachtkabarett, part of a programme in celebration of Guido Thielscher 50th birthday [Thielscher dancegirl] One performance on 27 March 1928 Lustspielhaus, Berlin.

It's in the Air/Es Liegt in der Luft by Marcellus Schiffer and Mischa Spoliansky, dir: Robert Forster Larrinaga [featured artist] Berlin, 15 May 1928.

Misalliance/Eltern und Kinder by George Bernard Shaw, dir: Heinz Hilpert [Hypatia Tarleton] Berlin, 12 September 1928

The Marquis of Keith/Der Marquis von Keith by Frank Wedekind, dir: Leopold Jessner [a guest], Berlin, 28 March 1929.

Two Bow Ties/Zwei Krawatten by Georg Kaiser and Mischa Spoliansky, dir: Forster Larrinaga [Mabel] Berlin, 5 September 1929.

FILM CREDITS

The dates listed below are the release dates of the films.
Years mentioned previously in the text refer to the time of production.

Wilhelm Dieterle's *The Man by the Roadside/Der Mensch am Wege* – June, 1923 Osmania-Film, Berlin (Production: April–May, 1923) [a peasant girl].

Joe May's *Tragedy of Love/Tragödie der Liebe* – October 1923 May-Film, Berlin (Production: spring 1922) [Lucie, the girlfriend].

Georg Jacoby's *The Little Napoleon/Der Kleine Napoleon* – November 1922 Europäische Film-Alianz, Berlin (UFA) (Production: June–November 1923) [walk-on].

Dr Johannes Guter's *The Leap Into Life/Der Sprung ins Leben* – January 1923, produced Erich Pommer Messter-Film, UFA, Berlin (Production: July–August 1923) [girl on beach].

Alexander Korda's My Wife's Dancing Partner/ Der Tänzer Meiner Frau – November 1926, Felson-Film, UFA, Berlin (Production 1926) [dancing extra].

Arthur Robinson's *Manon Lescaut* – February 1926, UFA, Berlin (Production: June–September 1925) [Micheline, Parisian courtesan].

Alexander Korda's *Madame Wants No Children/Madame wünscht keine Kinder* – December 1926, Deutche Vereins-Film AG, Berlin (Production: October–November 1926) [bit part].

Alexander Korda's *A Modern Dubarry/Eine Dubarry von Heute* – January 1927, Fellner & Somlo for UFA, Berlin (Production: April–August 1926) [credited as Marlaine, a French coquette].

Dr Willi Wolff's *The Imaginary Baron /Der Juxbaron* – March 1927, Ellen-Richter-Film Production, Berlin (Production: October-November 1926) [Sophie, the daughter].

Dr Willi Wolff's *Heads Up, Charly!/Kopf hoch, Charly!* – March 1927, Ellen-Richter-Film Production, Berlin (Production: autumn 1926) [Edmée Machand].

Harry Piel's *His Greatest Bluff/Sein grösster Bluff* – May 1927, Nero Film, Berlin (Production: January–February 1927) [Yvette, a prostitute].

Gustav Ucicky's *Café Electric/Café Elektrik* aka *When a Woman Loses Her Way/Wenn ein Weib den Weg verliert* – March 1928, Sascha-Film, Austria (Production: summer 1927) [Erni Götlinger].

Hermann Böttcher's *Princess Olala/Prinzessin Olala* – September 1928, Super Film, Berlin (Production: 1928) [Chichotte de Gastoné, lead].

Robert Land's *I Kiss Your Hand, Madame/Ich küsse Ihre Hand, Madame* – January 1929, Super Film, Berlin (Production: December 1928) [Laurene Gerard, lead].

Kurt Bernhardt's *The Woman One Longs For* aka *Three Loves/Die Frau, nach der man sich sehnt* – April 1929, Terra Film, Berlin (Production: January–February 1929) [Stascha, lead].

Maurice Tourneur's *The Ship of Lost Men/Das Schiff der verlorenen Menschen* – September 1929 Max-Glass-Film Production, Berlin (Production: April–June 1929) [Ethel Marley, lead].

Fred Sauer's *Dangers of the Engagement Period/Gefahren der Brautzeit* – February 1929 Strauss Film, Berlin (Production: September–October 1929) [Evelyn, lead].

Josef von Sternberg *Screen Test for Der Blaue Engel* – October 1929 [She sang 'You're The Cream in My Coffee' and 'Wenn man auseinander geht'].

Josef von Sternberg's *The Blue Angel/Der Blaue Engel* – 1 April 1930, UFA, Berlin (Production: November–January 1930) [Lola Lola].

Josef von Sternberg's *Morocco* – November 1930, Paramount, USA (Production: July–August 1930) [Amy Jolly].

Josef von Sternberg's *Dishonored* – March 1931, Paramount, USA (Production: October–November 1930) [Mary/X-27].

Josef von Sternberg's *Shanghai Express* – February 1932, Paramount, USA (Production: August–November 1931) [Shanghai Lily].

Josef von Sternberg's *Blonde Venus* – September 1932, Paramount, USA (May–June 1932) [Helen Faraday].

Rouben Mamoulian's *Song of Songs* – July 1933, Paramount, USA (Production: February–March 1933) [Lily Czepanek].

Josef von Sternberg's *The Scarlet Empress* – May 1934, Paramount, USA (Production: Spring 1934) [Catherine II/Sophia Frederica].

Josef von Sternberg's *The Devil Is a Woman* – May 1935, Paramount, USA (Production: October 1923–January 1935) [Concha Perez].

Josef von Sternberg's *The Fashion Side of Hollywood* – Spring 1935, Paramount, USA (Production: February 1935) [with Kathleen Howard, Travis Banton, John Bennett, Carole Lombard, Marlene Dietrich, George Raft, Claudette Colbert, Mae West].

Frank Borzage's *Desire* – April 1936, production Ernst Lubitsch. Paramount, USA (Production: September–December 1935, 4–5 February 1936) [Madeleine de Beaupre].

Henry Hathaway's *I Loved a Soldier* (never completed), Paramount, USA (Production: 3 January–11 February 1936).

Richard Boleslawski's *The Garden of Allah* – November 1936, Selznick International (Production: April–July 1936) [Domini Enfilden].

Jacques Feyder's *Knight Without Armour* – September 1937, London Films, UK (Production: July–November 1936) [Alexandra].

Ernst Lubitsch's *Angel* – November 1937, Paramount, USA (Production: March–June 1937) [Maria Barker].

George Marshall's *Destry Rides Again* – November 1939, Production: Joe Pasternak Universal (Production: September–November 1939) [Frenchy].

Tay Garnett's *Seven Sinners* aka *Café of the Seven Sinners* – November 1940, Production: Joe Pasternak Universal (Production: July–September 1940)[Bijou].

René Clair's *The Flame of New Orleans* – April 1941, Production: Joe Pasternak Universal (Production: January–March 1941) [Claire Ledoux].

Raqoul Walsh's *Manpower* – July 1941, Warner Brothers (Production: March–May 1941) [Fay Duval].

Mitchel Leisen's *The Lady Is Willing* – February 1942, Charles K Feldman Group for Columbia (Production: August–October 1941) [Elizabeth Madden].

Ray Enricht's *The Spoilers* – May 1942, Charles K Feldman Group for Universal (Production: January–February 1942) [Cherry Malotte].

Lewis Seiler's *Pittsburgh* – December 1942, (Production: 1942) [Josie 'Hunky' Winters].

The Show Business at War aka *March of Time* Vol. IX Issue 10 – 1943 (Production: 1943) [Herself].

Eddie Sutherland's *Follow the Boys* – 1944 Charles K. Feldman Group for Universal (Production: 1943) [special appearance with, among many, Orson Welles].

Wilhelm Dieterle's *Kismet* aka *Oriental Dream* – August 1944, MGM, US (Production: October–December 1943) [Jamilla].

Georges Lacombe's *Martin Roumagnac* – December 1946, Alcine, France (Production: summer 1946) [Blanche Ferrand].

Mitchell Leisen's *Golden Earrings* August 1947, Paramount, US (Production: August–October 1946) [Lydia].

Billy Wilder's *A Foreign Affair* – July 1948, Paramount, US (Production: Berlin: August–September 1947, Studio: December 1947–February 1948) [Erika von Schlütow].

Fletcher Markle's *Jigsaw* aka *Gun Moll* – March 1949, Tower Production for United Artists, US (Production: winter 1948) [nightclub patron].

Alfred Hitchcock's *Stage Fright* – February 1950, Warner Brothers, UK (Production: May–September 1949) [Charlotte Inwood].

Henry Koster's *No Highway in the Sky* aka *No Highway* – August 1951, 20th Century Fox, UK (Production: October 1950–January 1951) [Monica Teasdale].

Fritz Lang's *Rancho Notorious* 1952, Fidelity Pictures for RKO (Production: 1952) [Altar Keane].

Michael Anderson's *Around the World in 80 Days* – October 1956, TODD-AO, US (Production: 1956) [hostess].

Samuel A. Taylor's *The Monte Carlo Story* – 1957, Titanus/Tan Film US (Italian Production summer/autumn 1957) [Maria de Crevecoeur].

Billy Wilder's *Witness for the Prosecution* – January 1958, Theme Pictures, US (Production: January–August 1957) [Christine Vole, lead].

Orson Welles's *Touch of Evil* – February 1958, Universal-International, US (Production: February–March 1957) [Tanya].

Stanley Kramer's *Judgment at Nuremberg* – December 1961, Roxlom Films for United Artists, US (Production: January–May 1961) [Madame Bertholt].

Louis Clyde Stoumen's *Black Fox* – September 1962 Arthur Steloff/Image Production for MGM, US (Production: 1962) [narrator].

Richard Quine's *Paris When It Sizzles* – April 1964, Richard Quine Production/Charleston Enterprises, US (Production: Autumn 1963) Audrey Hepburn, William Holden [guest star].

Clark Jones's *I wish you love – an evening with Marlene Dietrich* – TV Special 1 January 1973, BBC, Brentwod, (Production: 23–24 November 1972).

David Hemmings's *Just a Gigolo* – November 1978, Leguan Film, Germany (Production: December 1977–March 1978) [Baroness von Semering].

Maximilian Schell's *Marlene – a documentary* –February 1984 Oko-Film/Karel Dirka Film, Germany (Production: interviews September 1982–83) (voice).

Further Reading

Bach, Steven, *Marlene Dietrich: Life and Legend* (1992, Da Capo Press, London, 2000) – *an amazing and comprehensive study of Dietrich's life. The author studied with Josef von Sternberg and met with Dietrich.*

Bahl, Peter *Herold-Jahrbuch, vol. 6* (Verlag Degener & Co., Postfach, 2001) – *a thorough study of the Dietrich, Felsing and von Losch family trees with several previously unseen photographs, amongst them Tante Vally.*

Brown, Philip (compilation) *Marlene Dietrich: The Songbook* (Wise Publications, London 1997) – *14 songs chosen from Dietrich's repertoire, presented with lyrics, scores, comments, and an introduction.*

Dickens, Homer *The Films of Marlene Dietrich* (1968; reprint, Secaucus, New Jersey: The Citadel Press, 1980) – *a thorough collection of Dietrich's film, silent and sound, with good summaries, notes, and unbiased comments.*

Dietrich, Marlene *Ich bin, Gott sei Dank, Berlinerin* (Ullstein, Munchen, 2000): Dietrich, Marlene *My Life*, (trans: Salvator Attanasio; 1987, Weidenfeld and Nicolson, London, 1989) – *Dietrich's own colourful account of her life. The language in the book suffers from multiple translations. The original English manuscript was translated to German, into French and from this version back to English.*

Dietrich, Marlene, *Marlene Dietrich's ABC* (1961; reprint, Avon Book Division from New York: Doubleday and Company, 1962) – *'The Wit and Wisdom of one of the world's most wonderful women.'*

Felsing, Hasso, *Der Ewige Ausländer* (Ewertverlag, Lathen 2000) – *a biography by Dietrich's cousin, son of Uncle Willi and Tante Jolly.*

Higham, Charles, *Marlene: The life of Marlene Dietrich*, (W. W. Norton & Company, New York, 1977) – *Written in the 1970s. Higham interviewed many of Dietrich's contemporaries.*

Martin, W K *Marlene Dietrich* – in a series on: Lives of notable gay men and lesbians – (Chelsea House Publishers, New York 1994) – *a study of Dietrich's bisexuality.*

Monthly Newsletters on Marlene Dietrich from Stiftung Deutsche Kinemathe – Marlene Dietrich Collection Berlin – *a free email newsletter provided by the Marlene Dietrich Collection. Includes everything from pictures from the collection and dates of forthcoming Dietrich events, to articles and comments on Dietrich. Email: info@filmmuseum-berlin.de; www.filmmuseum-berlin.de*

Morley, Sheridan *Marlene Dietrich* (1976; reprint, Great Britain: Sphere Books Limited, 1978) – *includes conversations with Dietrich and an account of one of her stage shows.*

O'Conner, Patrick, *The Amazing Blonde Women: Dietrich's own style* (Bloomsbury, London, 1991) – *a beautiful illustrated book with many unusual photographs, advertisements, press-photos, snapshots, and studio portraits.*

Riva, Maria, *Marlene Dietrich*, (Alfred A. Knopf, New York, 1993) – *written by Dietrich's only daughter and published shortly after her death; filled with personal and private anecdotes about Dietrich's life.*

Riva, Peter and Jean Jacques Naudet, *Marlene Dietrich, Photographs and Memories* (Alfred A. Knopf, New York, 2001) – *a stunning illustrated book with photos, letters, and pictures of the objects and costumes in the Marlene Dietrich Collection Berlin.*

Seydel, Renate, *Marlene Dietrich: Eine Chronik ihres Lebens in Bildern und Dokumenten* (Henschelverlag, Berlin, 1984) – *an astonishing and extraordinary collection of Dietrich's life in pictures, documents, and interviews of her friends, colleagues, and acquaintances.*

Spoto, Donald *Dietrich* (Bantam, London, 1988) – *good interviews and information making this book unique.*

Sudendorf, Werner, *Marlene Dietrich* (München: DTV, 2001) – *written by the director at the Marlene Dietrich Collection in Berlin with new and interesting research.*

von Sternberg, Josef *Fun in a Chinese Laundry* (reprint, New York: The Macmillian Company, 1965) – *an entertaining and well-written biography by Dietrich's most important mentor.*

von Sternberg, Josef, *The Blue Angel*, (Lorrimer Publishing, London, 1968) – *The Blue Angel script in English with the wonderful treat of an introduction from JvS.*

Walker, Alexander *Dietrich* (New York: Harper & Row, Publishers, 1984), – *part of the text is a little dated, but the pictures are marvellous and well-produced. Dietrich managed to halt Walker's launch of the book; her marked-up copy of the book is kept in the Marlene Dietrich Collection.*

Weth, George A., *Ich will wat Feinet: Das Marlene Dietrich Kochbuch* (Ritten & Loening, Berlin, 2001) – *a cookbook of the dishes that Dietrich might have made. A sweet idea with a nice account of Dietrich's last years spent at home.*

Jacobsen, Wolfgang, Hans Helmut Prinzler and Werner Sudendorf (eds) *Film Museum* (Nicolai, Berlin, 2000) – *an extended survey of the German film industry and the Marlene Dietrich Collection housed at the Film Museum, Berlin.*

Jacobsen, Wolfgang, Hans Helmur Prinzler and Werner Sudendorf (eds) *Film Museum: The Exhibition* (Nicolai, Berlin, 2000) – *the catalogue for the collection at the Film Museum, Berlin, including the permanent Marlene Dietrich exhibition.*

Riva, David, *Marlene Dietrich, Her Own Song,* (Documentary) USA, 2002 – *Dietrich's grandson produced this documentary of interviews, images and stories of his grandmother's life.*

Bauer, Christian and Matt, *Das Zweite Leben der Marlene* (Documentary) (Germany, 1994) – *the arrival of the Marlene Dietrich collection to the Berlin Film Museum.*

Picture Sources

The author and publishers wish to express their thanks to the following sources of illustrative material and/or permission to reproduce it. They will make proper acknowledgements in future editions in the event that any omissions have occurred.

Photographs courtesy of Marlene Dietrich Collection, Film Museum Berlin; except p. 7, courtesy of Verlag Degener & Co, Inhaber Manfred Dreiss

Index